The

Reference

Shelf

Aging in America

Edited by Olivia J. Smith

The Reference Shelf
Volume 72 • Number 3

The H.W. Wilson Company
New York • Dublin
2000

The Reference Shelf

The books in this series contain reprints of articles, excerpts from books, addresses on current issues, and studies of social trends in the United States and other countries. There are six separately bound numbers in each volume, all of which are usually published in the same calendar year. Numbers one through five are each devoted to a single subject, providing background information and discussion from various points of view and concluding with a subject index and comprehensive bibliography that lists books, pamphlets, and abstracts of additional articles on the subject. The final number of each volume is a collection of recent speeches, and it contains a cumulative speaker index. Books in the series may be purchased individually or on subscription.

Library of Congress has cataloged this serial title as follows:

Aging in America / edited by Olivia J. Smith.
    p. cm.— (The reference shelf ; v. 72, no. 3)
    Includes bibliographical references and index.
    ISBN 0-8242-0984-2 (pbk)
    1. Aged—United States. 2. Aged—Care—United States. 3. Baby boom generation—United States. 4. Aging—Social aspects—United States. I. Smith, Olivia J. II. Series.

HQ1064.U5 A63398 2000
305.26'0973—dc21
    00-042629

Visit H.W. Wilson's Web site: www.hwwilson.com

Printed in the United States of America

Contents

Preface

Aging is a topic that effects virtually everyone. Aside from the roughly 13 percent of the U.S. population who are currently aged 65 or older, nearly everyone has a relative who is or will soon be old. And most of us, as faraway as the time may now seem, will live to reach old age, if we are lucky. It follows that experiences of aging in America are nearly as diverse as contemporary Americans themselves. W. Andrew Achenbaum, a historian who studies perceptions of aging, contends that "older people are more diverse than any other age group"—in health, temperament, financial situation, and level of engagement with life, among other characteristics. According to Achenbaum, this fact is one of three "universals of aging." The others, as delineated in his article "Perceptions of Aging in America" (*National Forum,* Spring 1998), are that "old age has always been considered the last stage of existence before death," and "attitudes toward age and aging are very mixed."

How then, given its enormity, does one begin to broach the topic of aging in America? One of the first questions we might ask is, when does old age begin? Even to this apparently simple inquiry we would likely get a variety of responses, depending on who we asked. Eligibility for membership in the AARP, the country's largest senior citizens group, begins at age 50. A behemoth advocacy and service-providing organization whose ranks are open to all Americans, the AARP's name alone reflects the difficulty of making generalizations about our country's older people. Formerly an acronym for the American Association of Retired Persons, AARP remains the organization's name, but the letters are now officially divorced from their association with those words. The change was enacted due to polls showing that 80 percent of baby boomers, a generation on the brink of senior citizenship, plan to continue working—either part-time, in a new career, or by starting their own business—after they "retire." Boomers themselves named age 80 as the starting point of old age, according to a poll mentioned in the *CQ Researcher* (July 31, 1998), as compared to age 51 for their parents, roughly the same age named by the AARP. In another poll quoted in the same article, age 70 was the most typical answer to the question, "At what age do you consider someone to be elderly?" A canvass of American teenagers—who, according to yet another survey, believe most elderly to be in poor health and financially insecure—would likely yield a different opinion.

These disparities reflect generational differences in attitudes, as well as differences in health and self-perceptions among older people themselves. Many articles distinguish between the "young-old" and the "old-old," terms first coined by Bernice Neugarten, a prominent gerontologist. The first designation generally refers to people between the ages of 65 and 74, who are often depicted in the media as vibrant and attractive, living it up on the golf course or strolling on the beach in their retirement years. The same description also fits many of the old-old, those over age 75, although the members of this group are more likely to suffer from disease, disability, or frailness, require nursing home care, and depend on government programs such as Social Security and Medicare. The oldest-old, those aged 85 and older, among whom these likelihoods are still more pronounced, are the most rapidly growing segment of the population in many industrialized countries. The sometimes stark differences between these three groups, all of whom could legitimately be labeled "old," accounts for some of the confusion about the situation of the elderly. For example, the predominant perceptions of the young-old, which hold them to be healthy and affluent, have provided fodder for those who seek to radically change the Social Security program; if older people are so well-off, these reformers argue, why do they need monthly Social Security checks and other forms of assistance from the government? Such opinions may reflect inadequate consideration of the generally greater needs of the old-old. Opponents of major Social Security reform counter that it is largely because of the Social Security system that poverty among elderly people of all ages, although it still exists, has receded to such an extent that perceptions of seniors as predominantly poor and needy have begun to change.

The challenge of addressing aging in America does not end with the question of when old age begins. Many of the articles and book excerpts collected in this volume express points of view that would seem to contradict one another. For instance, some experts complain that there is too much focus on those elderly who are sick and frail, and too few images of seniors aging well. Others cite a dearth of what they consider to be realistic depictions of aging people in the popular media, contending that only extraordinary older people seem to merit society's attention: the elderly marathon runners or skydivers, or former senator John Glenn, whose recent return to space at age 77 was trumpeted by the media. In another example, older Americans are statistically healthier and wealthier than ever before. In one frequently cited study, more retirees reported feeling happy than did members of any other age group. Yet ageism, a term originated in 1975 by gerontologist Robert N. Butler in his Pulitzer Prize-winning book *Why Survive?—Growing Old in America,* remains for now an indelible part of American culture. Polls have shown that many older people don't like being referred to as "old" or "elderly." As Mary Pipher writes in *Another Country* (excerpted in Section IV), "In this country it is unpleasant to be called old, just as it is unpleasant to be called fat or poor. The old naturally try to avoid being identified with an unappreciated group." Is it more remarkable that older people feel happy in spite of society's distaste for them as a group, or that ageism persists in a country where being old is perhaps not so horrible after all? Aging in America is a difficult topic to grasp because conflicting images and perceptions such as these are nearly all based to some degree on truth. Older people are variously healthy and sick, wealthy and poor, independent and in need of help, active and depressed, alone and adored by friends and family, enjoying life and feeling alienated in a culture in which older people are still largely marginalized.

This book provides an introduction to some of the major issues associated with aging, many of which, if taken separately, would provide more than ample material for volumes of their own. For instance, the recent debates and legislation surrounding Social Security and Medicare can not begin to be fully addressed in an anthology such as this. It might be obvious that much more can, and should, be said on all the subjects included here, and the articles are intended merely as a starting point. Among feature stories, news reports, and commentaries, I selected articles penned by older people in which they describe their own experiences of aging, as well as articles that discuss people's day-to-day lives. In general, aside from the main goal of providing readers with a broad range of information and perspectives, these selections were informed by my personal interest—for myself and, in the more immediate future, for my parents—in finding ways to accept and even look forward to this much-feared time in life. In her book *The Fountain of Age*, Betty Friedan writes of the possibility of moving beyond views of aging that involve either "simulation of or decline from youth" to engage the process of aging on its own positive terms. While some of the unpleasant realities faced by many of America's elderly are represented in this book, so is Friedan's optimism and her belief in the value of aging and older people.

Section I introduces issues raised by the "graying" of the world's population and the effects the increasing numbers of older people may have on American society, particularly in regard to governmental policy and the economy. This section also examines older workers and points to another paradox; while growing numbers of older people want to keep working after retirement, and demographers and Social Security experts speak adamantly of the need to keep people employed later in life, ageism is perhaps most overt in the workplace. Section II addresses the aging of the baby boom generation. The maturing of this group is already having marked effects on how older people are perceived by others, and on how they perceive themselves. Section III discusses a few of the choices available to the increasing numbers of people faced with providing care for an elderly parent, grandparent, or other relative. Section IV looks at perceptions of the elderly in America, providing a brief introduction to this complex social topic. Lastly, the articles in Section V describe a vacation adventure, a writing workshop, and an approach to aging that reflect a view of the later years as a time for new experiences.

For their help, guidance, and patience during the preparation of this book, I would like to thank Cliff Thompson, Denise Bonilla, Sandra Watson, Gray Young, Lynn Messina, Sara Yoo, and Miriam Helbok, of the H.W. Wilson Company's general publications department. Thanks also to Lane Savadove and Jane, David, and Adam Smith for their love and support. Lastly, thanks to authors Mary Pipher and Robert L. Kahn and their agents for making it possible for me to reprint their valuable work in this volume.

Olivia J. Smith
May 2000

I. Retirement, Aging Workers, and the U.S. Government

Editor's Introduction

Section I begins with a brief overview of questions arising in response to global aging, a relatively recent development in world history. In the frequently cited book *Gray Dawn* (1999), Peter G. Peterson notes that up until the industrial revolution, people aged 65 and over comprised approximately two to three percent of the world's population at any given time. Statistical predictions printed in *U.S. News & World Report* estimate that, in contrast, by the year 2050, one of every five people in the world will be age 60 or older. According to the book *Successful Aging* (1998), an excerpt of which is included in Section IV, in the U.S., people aged 75 and older are the fastest growing segment of the population. Societies worldwide are rushing to adjust to these profound changes in their demographic makeup. The first article in this section, "The Longevity Revolution" (*The UNESCO Courier*) by Robert Butler, is a good introduction to some of the concerns posed by global aging, ranging from the political and economic to the social. From this general starting point, the rest of the articles in Section I discuss dilemmas posed by the growing ranks of the elderly in the U.S.

In "Off Golden Pond" (*The New Republic*), Robert J. Samuelson tackles the interrelated issues of retirement and social security, providing a brief history of their development and subsequent entrenchment as social institutions in the U.S. over the course of the 20th century. Samuelson uses statistics as well as several important books, including the two mentioned in the first paragraph of this preface, to support his argument that Americans need to retire later to offset the crippling effects that Social Security payments for the baby boom generation will have on the federal budget and, by extension, the American economy. He calls the aging of America "one of the most profound—and possibly fearsome—social changes in our history" and urges specific reforms aimed at keeping Americans in the workplace later in life, which would keep people contributing to the economy while reducing the collective cost of Social Security.

Theodore Roszak's article, "The Aging of Aquarius—Retiring Boomers and the Politics of Compassion" (*The Nation*), adapted from his book *America the Wise* (1998), serves as an indirect response to the views put forth by Samuelson. Roszak contends that through volunteerism, retired baby boomers will make valuable contributions to the economy even if they are not earning paychecks. In the future, Roszak suggests, senior volunteer projects could be expanded and participation could be tied to Social Security benefits.

In "Ageing Workers," a writer for *The Economist* discusses the potential impact of global aging on the work force. Many of the world's most productive countries may soon face a shrinking labor pool due to large numbers of retiring workers, and this holds sobering implications for productivity and standards of living worldwide. While in the past many employers have strongly encouraged early retirement, companies may now need to develop ways to keep skilled, experienced workers in the ranks longer.

While experts tout the economic benefits to be gained from people working later in life, perhaps the clearest examples of ageism occur in the workplace. According to a few recent articles, this type of discrimination is striking people at progressively younger ages, reflecting a national obsession with youth that is being increasingly felt in the workplace. In "The End of the Workday II" (*The Nation*), Margaret Morganroth Gullette writes about the social costs of this rising "middle ageism" and briefly cites several potential remedies.

In "Hunger in America" (*The Nation*), Trudy Lieberman focuses on the lack of sufficient government assistance for those elderly who do not have the means to provide food for themselves. This group, Lieberman contends, remains largely forgotten as the public focuses on younger, more affluent older people in the prime of their retirement years. Although there are government programs in nearly every region of the country to provide meals for the poor and homebound, there is not enough funding to feed all those in need. As a result, many people go hungry.

The Longevity Revolution[1]

BY ROBERT BUTLER
THE UNESCO COURIER, JANUARY 1999

In the coming century, the human life span may rise as high as 120 years. What are the implications of an aging world?

Over the past hundred years a silent and unprecedented revolution in longevity has occurred: people living in the industrialized world have on average gained 25 years of life, thanks largely to reduction of deaths at childbirth and infancy, and to control of diseases associated with old age. This is nearly equal to life expectancy advances over the preceding 5,000 years. In many countries, the 85-plus age group is the most rapidly growing.

The next century may bring even more dramatic increases. Prevention and elimination of disease along with control over the aging process itself could push our life spans from a world average of 66 years today to closer to 110 or 120 years—what scientists believe to be our "natural life span" because many individuals have lived that long. Some scientists talk of pushing the boundaries further by gaining control over the genes that determine longevity.

But our enhanced life spans do not come without a price. As the demographic balance increasingly tips to the elderly, societies are seeing their cultural, political and economic orders put to the test.

Among the most basic questions facing us are: At a time when the welfare state is coming under attack, who will be responsible for the financial support of the aged, the state or the individual? Will the aging of societies lead to economic stagnation? Will the aged form a politically powerful minority and if so, what demands will that group make? In extending our time on this planet, will we also be able to maintain quality of life, or are we doomed to pass our later years in sickness, frailty and financial incertitude? Culturally, will some of the attention now concentrated on youth shift to the elderly? As women outlive men in most of the industrialized world, many of the challenges associated with old age are particularly pertinent to them.

Our greater longevity has brought fundamental changes to our lives in ways that we either take for granted or of which we are hardly aware. For example, in 1920, a 10-year-old in the U.S. only had a 40 percent chance of having two of his or her possible four

---

1. Article by Robert Butler from *The Unesco Courier* January 1999. Copyright © 1999 *The Unesco Courier.* Reprinted with permission.

grandparents alive. Today, that figure is 80 percent. Thus, despite romantic images of a tighter knit family of former days, in fact, today we have a much greater proportion of multi-generational families than ever before.

In many ways, life is improving for the aged. For example, in the 1950s the average age of admissions into nursing homes was 65. Now the age is closer to 81. Today, older people in industrialized countries also have more choices about how they live: assisted living, home care or community-based care, for example. Morbidity rates are falling as a result of progress against heart disease and stroke.

"Silver Industries" to Cater for the Over-50s

One of the most fundamental issues is how to support the aged financially. Different societies have come up with different approaches. Despite its current economic difficulties, Japan adheres to a system under which the state provides for institutional and home care of the elderly. The United States is leading the way in a profit-oriented, managed care system, which emphasizes primary care, disease prevention and monitoring of distribution. However, the U.S. is not going far enough nor moving rapidly enough given the trajectory of old age. Meanwhile, the former Soviet Union has made major cutbacks in health care while slashing pension benefits as well.

So far much of our thinking about the aged has focused on them as a financial burden. But that attitude ignores fundamental facts that suggest to some extent that the very opposite is true. Today the U.S. pension funds amount to $2.7 trillion. This is money that helps provide capital for investment in production of goods and services, everything from roads to computer software start-ups. Overall, in the U.S., pension funds account for a quarter of all capital formation.

We must also remember that the aged represent an important group of consumers with very specific needs. Thus, in Japan, for example, a range of "silver industries" has grown up to cater to the housing, travel, recreation and other needs of those over 50. Similarly, in the U.S. companies talk increasingly about the senior or mature market. In recognition of the potential of this market, a number of publishers and electronic community builders have set up Internet Web sites targeted at the aged, complete with advertisements aimed at winning their custom. Meanwhile, in attempting to add to their bottom lines, pharmaceuticals companies increasingly concentrate on needs of the elderly: in industrialized countries those over 65 constitute roughly 15 percent of the population but account for some 30 percent of pharmaceuticals used.

Politically, the elderly will become a more powerful group with whom political parties in democratic countries at least will have to reconcile their policies. In the U.S., for example, the "baby boomers," born between 1946 and 1964 will begin to retire in the year 2008. In the decade beginning from 2020, they will constitute 20 percent of the U.S. population and as much as 30 percent of the electorate. Political candidates will no doubt have to pay increasing attention to their needs.

As societies struggle to address the challenges of aging populations, mere reorganization of the services to the elderly is no longer adequate. We require a redesign of the way we approach the needs of the elderly. In order for redesign to take place, some of our basic assumptions about the nature and character of old age must be questioned. This is already happening. Beginning in the 1950s, industrialized society began to perceive old age not as a period of life that is biologically fixed, but as one that is mutable.

The Feel-Good Factor

There are a number of reasons for these changing views. For one, the self-image of the aged has been changing. Increasingly, they now see themselves as vibrant and energetic and are not willing to let life end at retirement. Secondly, gerontologists now have a better understanding of the underlying mechanism of aging itself. This is leading to an appreciation of the possibility and reality of interventions, both preventative and therapeutic.

The growing demographic weight of the elderly is forcing us to reevaluate many of our old views. Since people are living longer, should they not work longer as well? To that question I would give a qualified yes. In the U.S., if we do not change our attitudes, we may by around the year 2020 have some 60 million idle people in retirement not contributing to society. We cannot afford to have so many people idle. Passage of the Age Discrimination Act in 1988 was a step forward as it no longer made retirement dependent on age itself. The market place has already absorbed millions of women and minorities, so there is no reason why jobs should not be found for older people as well.

Yet there are still many challenges ahead of us. The developing world has not generally enjoyed the same increase in longevity and decreased birth rates that have been seen in industrialized countries. Sixty percent of persons over the age of 60 currently live in the developing world and this is expected to increase to 80 percent by around the year 2025. Thus, there will be profound social, economic and political consequences of the aging revolution in all world regions.

Off Golden Pond[2]

The Aging of America and the Reinvention of Retirement

BY ROBERT J. SAMUELSON
THE NEW REPUBLIC, APRIL 12, 1999

I.

I am 53, and so I am in the vanguard of one of the most profound—and possibly fearsome—social changes in our history: the aging of America. Until 1980, the United States was a country of the young. The median age had hardly ever exceeded 30, meaning that half of the population was younger than 30 and half was older. For most of the nineteenth century, the median age was 20 or less. Between 1940 and 1980, it fluctuated within a narrow band between 28 and 30. Barring some calamity that devastates the elderly, we shall almost certainly never see 30 again. In 1997, the median age was nearly 35, and under plausible assumptions it will approach 39 by 2030. In later years, it could go higher.

Almost everyone is aware of these trends, which reflect lengthening life expectancy and declining birth rates. In 1950, those 65 and over were only 8 percent of the population, and they were a quarter the size of the 20-and-under group (34 percent). Even today, the 65-and-overs (13 percent) are less than half the 20-and-unders (29 percent). By 2030, however, applying those same plausible assumptions, the two groups will be roughly equal. Those 65 and over will be about 20 percent, compared with 24 percent for those 20 and under.

We all know that this change is coming, and yet we have done little—as a nation—to prepare for it; and we have only dimly contemplated what it means for our politics, our economy, and the character of our society. We imagine the future mostly as an extension of the present. All we need to do is to save more as individuals and, somehow, to ensure the survival of Social Security and Medicare, the main federal programs that support older Americans. With these precautions, we members of the baby boom can expect to retire in our early or middle 60s and proceed to enjoy our "golden years." Yet the future may not be an extension of the present. More important, the future must not be an extension of the present.

What we have done is to encourage people to retire at younger and younger ages—with vast public subsidies—even though they are healthier than ever and live longer than ever. Retirement has evolved from a short and necessary evil—a period in which people could no longer work and earn their way—into a sanctioned and cherished reward: a time to relax and to savor the pleasures of family, travel, hobbies, and leisure. For half a century, government policy and social custom have encouraged this increasingly sharp demarcation between "work" and "retirement." This may have made sense when people were sicker and life expectancy was shorter. But now it surely does not make sense; and if it is perpetuated, it may deaden the economy, poison politics, and breed nasty social resentments.

Retirement has evolved from a short and necessary evil—a period in which people could no longer work and earn their way—into a sanctioned and cherished reward.

We are, for starters, mortgaging our future. In their present form, Social Security, Medicare, and other government programs for the elderly will become hugely expensive for tomorrow's workers. The costs are so large that they threaten slowly to subordinate almost everything else that the federal government does—from national defense to national parks—to the need to pay for retirement programs. The Congressional Budget Office has done projections. They are only crude guesses, and they are subject to all the usual uncertainties about the future; but because they are based on fairly firm population trends, the basic outline is not mere speculation. And the numbers are sobering.

In 1998, the federal government spent 20 percent of national income (Gross Domestic Product), and the budget was roughly in balance. A third of spending already goes to the two largest programs for older Americans, Social Security and Medicare (health insurance for the 65-and-overs). The CBO projects their costs to almost double by 2030—from 7 percent of GDP now to 12 percent of GDP. Nor is that all. Medicaid—the federal-state health care program for the poor—now pays for almost 40 percent of all nursing-home care. With more people in nursing homes, Medicaid is projected to double from 1 to 2 percent of GDP by 2030. Probably half or more of this would go for the elderly.

So, put very crudely, we will spend about 13 percent of our national income on older Americans in a few decades. At present spending levels, this would be about two thirds of the budget. These projections could be optimistic; they presume that health costs come under control and that Congress does not pass new benefits for retirees. Even so, conflicts are unavoidable under highly favorable assumptions. Let's assume that the world remains a pretty safe place for Americans and that defense spending stays at 3 percent of GDP, its lowest level since 1940. Let's also assume that, over the next 15 years, we use budget surpluses to repay the publicly-held federal debt of $3.7 trillion. This helps, because interest on the debt now costs us about 3 percent of GDP.

Where does this leave us? Well, three quarters of the budget goes to defense, retirement programs, and Medicaid. That is about 17 percent of GDP. The rest of the federal government (scientific research, the FBI, school programs, food stamps, the Environmental Protection Agency) now costs about 6 percent of GDP. To stay within the present budget (20 percent of GDP), this spending would have to be squeezed by about half. Or we could raise taxes by 15 percent; in today's dollars, that would amount to about $250 billion a year. Or, finally, we could resume massive budget deficits.

The outlook is daunting, even under optimistic assumptions

The rigid separation between work and retirement is segmenting society into producers and parasites in ways that will ultimately benefit neither.

(which are probably unrealistic). And, of course, higher taxes or deficits might threaten prosperity by reducing economic growth. But this is not the only problem of an aging America. Suppose that we simply assume that the future is affordable, in the sense that higher taxes or deficits do not cripple the economy. Present policies are still leading in the wrong direction. They are promoting a new type of segregation between those who are responsible for keeping the country going and those who—to put it bluntly—live off its bounty. The rigid separation between work and retirement is segmenting society into producers and parasites in ways that will ultimately benefit neither.

I may not want to work full-time for another 20 years, but I doubt that I will want to stop cold turkey. A lot of people feel the same way. By some surveys, they would like to mix work and retirement. This is hard to do today. But regardless of what I want, it certainly will not be healthy for society to have me—and millions like me— step aside for the last 15 or 20 years of our lives. Most of us will not be incapacitated and unable to work. That will become glaringly obvious to those who are forced to work and pay for our leisure. It would be unnatural if they didn't resent us.

We need to reinvent retirement. It ought to be less rigid and more attuned to changing social and economic realities. This does not mean abandoning today's system, including Social Security and Medicare. It does mean refashioning these programs. Since we live longer and are healthier, retirement ages should be raised to 68, and perhaps to 70. Since the old are wealthier, we should reduce benefits for the well-to-do and focus more on the poor. These steps would curb costs and encourage people to work longer, perhaps through part-time or part-year jobs. If we subsidize early retirement less, we will get less of it. The changes should be gradual, to give people ample time to prepare.

Whether we can accomplish this reinvention is unclear. Modern retirement is a huge social triumph, and Social Security and Medicare underpin that triumph. Their success transcends mere popularity. They helped the nation cope with social conditions that were barely foreseeable when these programs were created. Hardly anyone thought in 1935—the year in which Congress passed the Social Security Act—that life expectancy would leap forward so rapidly. In 1930, life expectancy at birth was 60; today it is 76. Even in 1965, when Congress enacted Medicare, the sense that most Americans would experience an extended retirement was weak.

Modern retirement is a huge social triumph, and Social Security and Medicare underpin that triumph.

Many Americans could not or did not save for their retirements, because they could not have plausibly anticipated that they would live so long. Social Security and Medicare compensated. They enabled many workers—especially men—to retire before their bodies broke down. Millions of others were spared from having to throw themselves on the mercy and charity of families. The paradox is that, although the elderly became more heavily dependent on government, these federal programs helped them feel more self-sufficient economically and psychologically.

The trouble is that the independence is a myth. Retirees remain massively dependent on government. Yet this myth has created expectations and constituencies that obstruct any revision of retirement. Almost all the talk of "reforming" Social Security and Medicare—or "saving" them—misses the reforms that are genuinely needed. Those reforms are largely off-limits politically, because they would reduce benefits by making them available later and focusing them more on the poor. Few politicians will touch these questions. A prudent society would do so; it would have done so ten or fifteen years ago. But we are not being prudent.

II.

How we reached this point is largely a forgotten story. What has become a political and psychological entitlement—a long and rewarding retirement—did not spring full-blown from the Social Security Act or any single event. It emerged slowly from rising prosperity, improving health, and a growing welfare state. A century ago, most men worked until they could no longer do so. Many died before they reached today's retirement age. At the age of 20 in 1900, white men could expect to live only until their early 60s. For blacks at the same age, life-spans averaged about a decade less. Women (also at 20) lived only a few years longer than men, and most were not wage earners. The decisive and terrifying event of their old age was often widowhood.

Dora L. Costa recounts (in a dry, academic prose) how all this changed. Her major contribution is to show that, even without Social Security and Medicare, retirement would have expanded dramatically. Indeed, by some statistics, the largest increases occurred before Social Security became important. In 1880, 78 percent of men 65 and over worked. By 1940, this had dropped to 44 percent. In 1990, it was 18 percent. By this measure, more than half the increase in men's retirement preceded the explosion of Social Security spending in the 1950s and 1960s. If nothing else, this attests to a deep longing to be free of toil, because—as Costa shows—men's health improved over this period. People were not less able to work; they simply worked less.

For a few reasons, this overstates the early expansion of retirement. Since retirement was such an alien concept, few good historical statistics exist. So Costa is driven to equate retirement among men with the statistical condition of not having a job after age 65. The two are different. Early in the century, older men were often fired and couldn't find new jobs. In the Great Depression, this surely accounted for a big rise in "retirement." And then there is what comes before and after age 65. Most workers now retire before 65. In 1995, 58 percent of workers took Social Security benefits at age 62, and 20 percent more took them at ages 63 and 64. Early retirement hardly existed in the 1950s. Congress did not authorize Social Security benefits at 62 until 1956 for women and until 1961 for men. And now people live longer, so retirement lasts longer. Since 1950, average life expectancy at age 65 has risen three years for men (to 16) and four years for women (to 19). All this means that the major expansion of retirement has occurred since World War II.

Still, Costa's central point survives: retirement's expansion transcends government policy. It has a power all its own. Private pensions, for example, started at American Express in 1875. By 1930, about 10 percent of the private labor force (2.7 million workers) were covered by some pension. The Revenue Act of 1942—a major wartime tax bill—made most contributions to company pensions tax-deductible. During the war, companies sometimes provided future pension benefits as a way to evade wage controls. The long-run effect was to foster more pensions, but even without the tax subsidy they would have spread.

In those early years, though, the idea of retirement was different. As Costa notes, the first private and government pension programs reflected many motives, but none embodied a belief that people deserved a period of rest, reflection, and enjoyment before death. Those were other times with other values, other customs, other con-

---

. . .the first private and government pension programs reflected many motives, but none embodied a belief that people deserved a period of rest, reflection, and enjoyment before death.

---

cerns. Indeed, the very notion of organized and commercialized leisure was novel a century ago. In 1910, fewer than 30 percent of male workers had a recognized vacation, and most of that was unpaid. Rest and recreation were not things that were thought to be owed to people. And government aid to the old, the poor, and the disabled was meager or non-existent.

True, Congress did create a pension program for Union veterans after the Civil War, and eventually the program was extended to their widows. In the late nineteenth and early twentieth centuries, benefits went to nearly 1 million people and represented 25 to 30 percent of all federal spending. About a quarter of the 65-and-over population was covered. Yet the program was justified only as an expression of national gratitude to soldiers. Social reformers hoped that the military pensions would act as a springboard for a universal program. In 1909, one reformer wrote: "The nation [has] already declared it to be our duty to shelter the aged and wounded soldier, why should the victims of the 'army of labor' be neglected." The hope went unrealized.

A few states did create pensions. Arizona was the first, in 1915, though a court later threw out the program. Nevada, Montana, and Pennsylvania—states with "small elderly populations," Costa says—passed programs in 1923. Not until the Depression did many states do so. By the end of 1934, 28 states had programs, including Arizona. But benefits were small, while income and residency requirements were stiff. As Costa observes, "pensions could be denied to those who had financially responsible relatives, failed to work when judged capable, had deserted their families, were tramps or beggars, disposed of their property to qualify for a pension, were recipients of other government pensions, or were inmates." Those eligible for benefits ranged from 1 percent of the elderly in Maryland to 22 percent in Arizona.

Humanitarian and pragmatic concerns prompted these programs. Somehow, the needs of workers who couldn't handle jobs had to be met. In 1919, the Ohio Health and Old Age Insurance Commission observed: "Very few wage-earners can expect to be able to work until the end of their lives. . . . How are they to obtain a livelihood during those last years of life? This is the problem of old age as it affects the working-man." The same sensibility shaped the Social Security Act. The law dealt with "economic security" and also created federal-state programs for unemployment insurance and aid to single mothers.

Indeed, the largest program for the elderly was not the present system of Social Security, which did not pay out its first benefit until 1940. It was an old-age assistance program that joined with state programs to help the poorest of the elderly. Again, the motive was simple decency, compounded by a desire—understandably strong in the Depression—to encourage the hiring of younger workers by making it easier for older workers to quit or to be fired. In upholding the law, Supreme Court Justice Benjamin Cardozo wrote that "the hope behind this statute is to save men and women from the rigors of the poorhouse as well as from the haunting fear that such a lot awaits them when journey's end is near."

We have come a long way from these modest beginnings. One reason is that, over the years, Congress periodically increased benefits. In 1950, a retiring worker with average earnings received Social Security payments equal to about 20 percent of pre-retirement earnings. (This ratio is known as the replacement rate.) Now, benefits for a worker with average earnings amount to about 43 percent of pre-retirement earnings. For low-wage workers (those with 45 percent of average wages), the replacement rate is now about 58 percent, up from 33 percent in 1950. In practice, these figures understate the true comparison, because all Social Security benefits were untaxed until 1983, and most still are untaxed. So the replacement rate on after-tax income is higher.

Beyond this, the creation of Medicare in 1965 covered much of the elderly's health costs and, just as important, diminished the fear that they would be impoverished by unexpected medical bills.

Pensions and private savings have also increased over the years. In 1996, they provided about 40 percent of income for the 65-and-over population (more for the well-to-do than the poor). By and large, older Americans now live on their own, whether in retirement communities or not. This, too, represents a gradual change. In 1880, almost half of retired men over 65 lived with children or relatives. Even in 1940, about a fifth (22 percent) did. Now, only about 5 percent do.

The result is that retirement has now become more a lifestyle and a choice, and less a sign of incapacity. And it is socially acceptable to acknowledge this fact. In 1951, only 3 percent of retiring men said "they had retired because they preferred leisure to work," Costa writes. By 1982, this was 48 percent. There is strength in numbers. As retirement has become more popular and respectable, it has also become more appealing, because there is more to do. For "seniors," there are retirement communities, exercise groups, travel tours, and discounts of all varieties. Virtually all the advances of modern technology—air travel, better highways and cars, cable television, and now the Internet—give the retired more opportunities. Costa quotes one retiree from a study conducted in the late 1970s:

> My wife and I have completely changed our lifestyle since retirement. For the first couple of years we traveled around the country to see sights and country (historical and scenic) I wanted to see. Then we joined the Wally Byam Caravan Club International and have greatly enjoyed new friends and a new lifestyle. We live in a 31-foot airstream trailer—spend seven months in winter in a park in Melbourne, Fl., where we have every kind of activity. We dance and square dance and party all winter. Then in summer we travel around—stop and spend some days with children and grandchildren and the rest of the time traveling to rallies in caravans and sightseeing from Canada through 48 states and Mexico.

"The retired have become the true leisured class," writes Costa. That is an understatement.

III.

Unless you disapprove of pleasure, it is hard to object. The idea that we can, while still healthy and vigorous, cruise the country, visit children and grandchildren, read, play golf—or simply escape the daily grind—is enormously seductive to most people. Early retirement has risen because people like it. Still, there can be too much of a good thing, and that is what modern retirement is becoming. The trouble, again, is that all this leisure is hugely subsidized. Almost all older Americans, even the well-off, rely heavily on Social Security and Medicare. Among the richest fifth of people 65 and over, Social Security was 21 percent of their income in 1996. Among the second richest, it was 47 percent. As with all subsidies, we need to ask: Who gets? Who pays? And who benefits—society or merely the beneficiaries?

For years, we have dodged these urgent but delicate questions by means of a variety of ingenious rationales. We deny the very concept of subsidy by insisting that retirement benefits were "saved" for recipients or, more vaguely, "earned." These beliefs are delusions. Social Security is a pay-as-you-go program. Current taxes pay current benefits, even though the money passes through a "trust fund." The same is true of Medicare (though only part of its money flows through a "trust fund"). The past payroll taxes of today's beneficiaries were not "saved" to pay their benefits. Social Security benefits are related to earnings, but the relationship is weak. Benefits are proportionately higher for low-income workers. Retirees receive welfare payments just as food-stamp recipients do. Congress has decreed that a class of people deserve benefits and has set the criteria for eligibility.

We deny the very concept of subsidy by insisting that retirement benefits were "saved" for recipients or, more vaguely, "earned."

"Welfare" is a pejorative term in America, and so hardly anyone applies it to Social Security or Medicare. Almost everyone feels sympathy toward the old. With luck, we all expect to become old; and today's old are usually someone's parents or grandparents. This general feeling of goodwill has insulated Social Security and Medicare from criticism and change. But rising costs are eroding this immunity. For this reason, we are hearing new arguments about why we need not worry: faster economic growth can pay the costs of the baby boom; so can greater immigration; and the costs have been exaggerated because society's dependency ratio (the combination of young and old) is not increasing.

Peter G. Peterson does not believe any of these arguments. He is an admitted alarmist on aging, having written three previous books on the same general subject. *Gray Dawn* has two main virtues. The first is to show that the problems in Europe and Japan are worse than the problems in the United States. Their populations are aging more rapidly, in part because their families have fewer children. In the United States, the fertility rate (the number of children per woman) is about 2, which replaces the population. But it is 1.4 in Japan, 1.3 in Germany, and 1.2 in Italy. As a result,

Italy will have a fifth of its population 65 or over by 2003, Japan by 2005, and Germany by 2006. In some countries, work forces will soon shrink.

The book's second virtue is to refute all the reasons that we have been given not to worry. Begin with the economy: if we expand the pie faster, we are told, everyone can have a bigger piece. This sounds easy, but it is virtually impossible. Economic growth stems mainly from two factors: more workers (or longer hours); and higher productivity (efficiency, or output per hour worked). Since 1960, roughly half of the economy's growth has stemmed from expansion of the labor force. Between 1960 and 1998, workers grew from 70 million to 138 million. But the retirement of the baby boom will slow the growth of the labor force to a crawl after 2015. So productivity would have to double or more—possible, but unlikely—to maintain present economic growth. And even that would be a mixed blessing. Faster productivity growth would mean higher wages; and with Social Security benefits tied to wages, benefits would also ulti- mately rise.

What about immigration? It might help slightly, with the empha- sis on "slightly." At present, legal and illegal immigration probably exceeds 1 million a year. Peterson estimates that this might have to rise to 4 million annually to make a sizeable impact on paying for federal retirement programs. Even if his estimate is high, common sense suggests that the point is correct. To make a difference, immi- gration would have to be huge. But this would, in turn, magnify the social strains of assimilating waves of newcomers. There is little public desire for this. "In America, as throughout the developed world, a growing share of voters wants to restrict immigration *beneath* current levels," Peterson rightly remarks.

Finally, there is the dependency ratio. It simply defines the prob- lem away. Together, the burden of the young and old—those depen- dent on others—will not change; and so (the argument goes) the future will be as affordable as the past. In 1970, those younger than 20 were 38 percent of the population and those 65 and over were 10 percent. That amounts to 48 percent. In 2030, the two are projected to amount to 44 percent (20 percent for the old, 24 percent for the young). But not so fast, says Peterson. Families pay directly most of the costs of children, while government (and, therefore, taxation) bears the burden of the elderly. In 1995, federal, state, and local government spent about $15,000 for every American over 65 and about $6,000 (including school) for every child. And there's another crucial difference: "Money spent on children is an investment [in society's future]."

So the aging problem will not fade away. Faster economic growth and more immigration might ease the stresses; but the stresses are immutable. Peterson also discards another solution: "privatization." That label covers many proposals that would replace or supplement Social Security with private savings accounts, financed with payroll taxes. The idea is that workers would save for their own retirements. Although Peterson isn't hostile, he rightly notes that this approach will not save the baby boom. It is too late. Unless Congress reduced or eliminated benefits for today's recipients, there is not enough money to finance savings accounts for the baby boom that would pay benefits at promised levels. Any privatization would have to cut current benefits or be phased in over many decades. Initially, extra taxes might be needed to finance the savings accounts.

Thus the irresistible force (aging population) is meeting the immovable object (retirement programs). Sooner or later, a collision is inevitable. The only question is whether it occurs sooner or later. The evidence from abroad is not reassuring. In 1995, Peterson reports, "the Dutch Parliament was forced to repeal a recently enacted cut in retirement benefits after a strong Pension Party, backed by the elderly, emerged from nowhere to punish the reformers. In 1996, the French government's modest proposal to trim pensions triggered strikes and even riots." Political paralysis is widespread.

By income, the old are much poorer than the young.

We ought to remember that stalemate creates winners and losers. Government retirement programs involve massive income redistribution from the young to the old. Increasingly, this is also a transfer from a poorer and less economically secure population to a richer and more secure one. By income, the old are much poorer than the young. In 1996, households 65 and over had a median income of $29,000, compared to $48,000 for households 35 to 44 and $57,000 for households 45 to 54. But this comparison is misleading, though it is often made. Median net wealth (the value of what people own—their homes, stocks, cars—minus their debts) is usually higher for the old than the young. In 1995, it was $107,000 for those 65 to 74 compared with $51,000 for those 35 to 44 and $91,000 for those 45 to 54.

More important, older Americans say in surveys that they feel more secure. The National Opinion Research Center asks respondents whether they are "satisfied," "more or less satisfied," or "not at all satisfied" with their financial situation. In 1998, 43 percent of those 65 and over said they were satisfied and only 14 percent said they were not. This exceeded every other age group. Among those 40 to 49, only 27 percent pronounced themselves satisfied, while 28 percent said they were not. There are many possible explanations for these age-related differences. Living expenses for older Americans are generally lower. Almost four-fifths own their homes, most probably with mortgages paid. Child-rearing costs have shriveled, as have work expenses. Taxes are lower. Income—from Social Security, pensions, savings—may seem more stable. People's ambitions are lower.

Still, the irony is inescapable. It is doubtful that the architects of Social Security or Medicare anticipated that they were creating programs that would transfer huge amounts from a less economically secure group to a more economically secure group. But these programs have succeeded so spectacularly—and the well-being of the elderly has improved so dramatically—that this is increasingly occurring.

IV.

Aging societies around the world pose profound questions. Will they become economically moribund, because the old are less inventive and less accepting of change? How will families cope if people have to care for both their children and their parents who, increasingly, live to 85, 90, or 100? How will we deal with the ethical issues of prolonging life at great expense and little hope? Will the world become more dangerous, because older societies—with few children—will not risk their youth in war and will become vulnerable to those that will? Peterson poses all these questions and answers none of them, because they are unanswerable. We cannot predict the future.

But we are not powerless to affect the future. We can deal with the obvious problems. Many possible solutions are no mystery. In its recent report, the Congressional Budget Office outlines some of them. One is to raise the eligibility ages for Social Security and Medicare. Already Social Security's normal retirement age of 65 is scheduled to move gradually to 66 by 2009 and stay there until 2020 (affecting those born between 1943 and 1954). Then it would rise slowly to 67 by 2027 for those born in 1960 or after. These increases could be accelerated. My own view is that we should move to 68 by 2015 or 2020, and then maybe to 70. Existing law would preserve Social Security at 62, though with reduced benefits. I would raise this threshold; and I would also raise Medicare's eligibility along with Social Security's.

Similarly, benefits could be skewed more toward poorer recipients. The existing formula already does this. In 1997, for example, it replaced 90 percent of new retirees' monthly earnings up to $455, but only 15 percent above $2,741. By tinkering with the formula, benefits in the upper half of the income distribution could be cut. The 65-and-over population also receives special tax breaks, mainly the exclusion of most Social Security benefits from taxes. In 1999, these are worth more than $20 billion. These should be phased out. And older Americans—especially the affluent—could be asked to bear more of the costs of Medicare. Today, Medicare premiums cover only about 11 percent of expenses.

Such proposals could be mixed in various combinations. Almost any plan would sharply reduce future budget costs. The Congressional Budget Office estimated that the savings from a more modest package (less increase in the retirement age, for instance) might keep the budget in balance over the next 75 years (assuming a constant level of taxes and other spending as a share of GDP). But cutbacks also have a second purpose: to extend peoples' working lives by making earlier retirement less attractive. As Peterson writes: "Working longer is not a way to avoid the hard choices. It *is* the hard choice."

Working longer does not mean that people will stay in career jobs for another three, four, or five years. Some will, but some will not want to—and some will not be able to. Corporate "downsizing" in the past decade hurt workers most in their late 40s, 50s, and early 60s. Companies in trouble are often in mature industries, and therefore have older work forces. Economic logic also induces companies to nudge out older workers, who are put at a disadvantage by seniority-based pay systems and fringe benefit costs. Peterson quotes the management consultant Sylvester Schieber: "In the U.S., we have a major problem in our pay structure being related to age. . . . Employer-financed health costs are higher for older workers. Leave programs award workers with longer tenures for time not worked. . . . Disability and workers' comp costs rise with age. All of these facets of the pay system reduce older workers' relative profitability."

If older workers have to be paid near the top of the pay scale, many companies will not hire them. Age discrimination laws need to take this into account.

So there are practical complications. If older workers have to be paid near the top of the pay scale, many companies will not hire them. Age discrimination laws need to take this into account. Nor should laws be drawn so tightly that companies can't dismiss workers who seem less productive or valuable. That would invite economic stagnation. Workers who lose career jobs—or quit because they are fed up after 20 or 30 years—may still need a job. But a new job may pay less than the old; and it might lack health insurance. Should people below 65 be allowed to buy Medicare coverage? If so, down to what age? At what price?

These practical problems, I think, can be overcome. The American economy has shown that it can generate new jobs and customize jobs to fit new groups of workers. Over the last 40 years, it has done so for two huge groups, women and teenagers, who have flooded the labor market. Why couldn't it do the same for older Americans? As labor-force growth slows—a consequence of societal aging—companies will surely seek to retain good workers. Firms might offer "staying" bonuses just as some now offer "signing" bonuses. Or they might design more part-time, part-year, or "consulting" jobs to accommodate a desire for more leisure.

We do not really need to know the precise answers. If the economy remains healthy—if there is no depression—we can assume that the demand for older workers will materialize. But what about supply? Will older Americans want to work? Probably not, if we continue paying them so much not to work. Our present programs, which started as a humane effort to aid people who couldn't work and were inevitably dependent, now encourage them to stop working when they still can. Lower subsidies would reverse that. People would have to earn more to pay for their retirements. This is probably the only way that most Americans will work longer.

Hardly anyone discusses these questions. President Clinton certainly is not discussing them. He has consistently refused to consider major benefits cuts—and he has attacked and undercut anyone who has considered them. His refrain is "saving" Social Security and Medicare. Congress, predictably, also will not touch the issue. Democrats regard Social Security and Medicare as political preserves. Republicans are terrified that any hint of a benefit cut (no matter how far in the future) will subject them to withering political attack. All the lobbies for older Americans protect benefits. And so there is a bipartisan consensus to do nothing. It could last for years, because the budgetary pressures of an aging society do not truly intensify for ten to fifteen years.

The problem with procrastination, of course, is that it will be hugely unfair to someone. As more people retire, it may be politically impossible to alter benefits. This would punish tomorrow's workers with higher taxes, lower government services, or higher federal debt. It is also possible that the costs of these programs will—when coupled with the impact of trends and events we cannot now foresee—become so heavy that Congress will be forced to cut benefits. This would punish baby-boom workers, who would have the rules of retirement changed in midstream, with little time to prepare.

President Clinton bears much of the blame for the present paralysis. One disappointment of Peterson's book is that he does not say so forthrightly. In 1994, Peterson served on the Commission on Entitlements and Tax Reform, appointed by Clinton. It urged action to curb spending, and Peterson blandly declares that "America's political leadership thanked us for the report, shook our hands, and walked away." No, it was Clinton who shook his hand and walked away. A President has the almost unique power to set the political agenda—to determine what issues will be debated, on what terms, and in what language. If a Democratic President will not acknowledge the need for benefit cuts, then Republicans will understandably shy away. When they bravely suggested cuts in Medicare in 1995, Clinton successfully—and dishonestly—savaged them.

Peterson writes as if he would still like to be invited to the White House. By soft-pedaling his criticism, he (and others like him) serve as enablers of this terrible procrastination. But there is a deeper cause of the present paralysis. Public opinion regards almost any discussion of cutting retiree benefits as inhumane, unprogressive, and even barbaric. Clinton panders to this climate and perpetuates it; but he did not create it. As long as it survives, debate will be stilled.

Public opinion regards almost any discussion of cutting retiree benefits as inhumane, unprogressive, and even barbaric.

The public's notion of aging subsists on an outdated image of retirees. Until now, I have depicted them as a cheerful, healthy, and secure bunch who frolic at everyone else's expense. This is wildly inaccurate, of course. A fifth of the 65-and-older population require some help in daily activities—dressing, getting about, eating. About 5 percent live in nursing homes. About 11 percent have incomes below the federal poverty line; and without Social Security, more than half might live below it. Older Americans have sharp and obvious anxieties. They fear loneliness, the death of a spouse, and the loss of self-sufficiency. They worry that they will become a burden on their children or that their children will abandon them. They dread going into a nursing home. They think about dying and the possibility that it will be prolonged, painful, and degrading.

Getting old isn't a picnic, but many of the worst medical and emotional problems do not occur until people reach their 70s or 80s. I have emphasized the opposite picture because it, too, is true—and it is ignored in our debates. We talk about old age as if nothing had changed since 1935 or 1965. As Costa reminds us, the retirement age of 65 dates back to Bismarck's pensions in the late nineteenth century. Yet political convention still considers this dividing line almost sacrosanct, pretending that everyone on one side is generally healthy, vigorous, and alert, and almost everyone on the other is frail, poor, and (sooner or later) feeble-minded.

We know from casual observation, common sense, newspaper stories (John Glenn rocketing into space), and research that this picture is false. And for those who distrust common sense or anecdotal evidence, the research is impressive. In 1987, the MacArthur Foundation began sponsoring an extensive study of the aging process by a variety of scholars. The results, summarized in *Successful Aging*, demolish the stereotypes. Here is one indicator of improved physical well-being: in 1957, 55 percent of the 65-and-older population had no teeth; now the figure is 20 percent. In general, the studies found that most people are physically and mentally fit well beyond 65. In 1994, 89 percent of those between 65 and 74 reported "no disability whatsoever." And the studies find that individuals' aging is affected more by lifestyle—diet, physical exercise, emotional connections—than heredity. (According to one study, the influence of genes is about 30 percent.)

It is long past time to conform political debate to social reality. We also need to reject the platitudes that the elderly can contribute to society by volunteering or offering "wisdom." This may be true, but it is a tiny truth. The main way that older Americans can contribute is by doing the same thing that other adults do: that is, by working, and not becoming a premature social burden. We need to abandon the notion that everyone over 65 is entitled to become a ward of the state. People do not suddenly become "needy" and dependent on their 65th birthday. I have always disliked the term "greedy geezers"—it is inflammatory and it stigmatizes an entire generation (mainly the Depression and World War II generation) for the good fortune of living long. But enough is enough. If baby-boom politicians perpetuate the status quo, we can be sure of one thing: our children will call us greedy geezers. And they will be right.

The Aging of Aquarius[3]

Retiring Boomers and the Politics of Compassion

By Theodore Roszak
The Nation, December 28, 1998

> In the March 25, 1968, issue of *The Nation* appeared the first of four articles by Theodore Roszak on what he dubbed the "counter culture." Roszak, then a history professor at California State College, expanded the articles into a book, *The Making of a Counter Culture,* published the following year. He was one of the first to recognize as a distinctive phenomenon the sixties youth movement, which embraced the New Left, the hippies, flower power, psychedelic drugs and rock music. Thirty years later, Roszak has written a new book, *America the Wise,* in which he speculates about the effects of the "new aging" and greater longevity on American society as the cohort he chronicled thirty years ago approaches retirement age. What follows is a representative excerpt.
>
> —*The Editors* [The Nation]

In the years ahead, an increasing number of us will be living decades longer than our parents or grandparents. Think of all those extra years of life as a *resource*—a cultural and spiritual resource reclaimed from death by advances in public health and medical science in the same way the Dutch reclaim fertile land from the waste of the sea. During any one of those years, somebody who no longer has to worry about raising a family, pleasing a boss or earning more money will have the chance to join with others in building a compassionate society where people can think deep thoughts, create beauty, study nature, teach the young to worship what they hold sacred, and care for one another. Once we realize that, we should have no difficulty understanding the most important fact about the longevity revolution. It has given the baby boomers now in their 50s—the remarkable generation I wrote about thirty years ago in *The Making of a Counter Culture*—a chance to do great good against great odds.

Many of the people we think of as "senior citizens" at the turn of the twenty-first century (what I shall call the middle old—people now in their 60s and 70s—and the senior old—those 80 to 100

---

plus) have retired into an empty space filled with card games or love-boat cruises. That is retirement as we have known it: a withdrawal into inconsequentiality. There are commercial forces at work that would delight in keeping things just that trivial and profitable.

This current generation of seniors—especially those in the middle-old range who have put aside some money—is already growing restless with a life limited to the card table and the golf course. As a sign of significant change, a distinctive new occupation has already grown up around that restlessness. It is called "volunteer vacationing."

Volunteer work has long been seen as a province of the elderly, whether as museum docents or hospital candy stripers. But the volunteering involved in these vacations is of a wholly different order. Indeed, the term "vacation" obscures the reality. This is actually rigorous public service, but with a novel twist. These public servants pay to work. They often lay out a good deal of their own money to cover the cost of transport, lodging, food and care. Environmental organizations like Earthwatch Institute and the National Audubon Society, as well as government agencies like the U.S. Forest Service and the Fish and Wildlife Service, have been making the most extensive use of senior volunteers. They now organize vacations that allow participants to do significant conservation work: repairing public facilities in wilderness areas, building trails, taking censuses of wildlife, planting and restoring parks. Sometimes the effort includes assisting on digs to find and catalogue fossil remains or preserve native habitats.

There are also inner-city vacations, like those of Habitat for Humanity, whose purpose is to build homes for the poor, and Third World vacations that demand substantial stamina. The American Hiking Society, for example, advertises vacations that involve "hard, manual labor in rugged, remote locations, many at high altitudes." Fortunately for older participants, the assignments are not restricted to heavy lifting. There are other opportunities for teachers, technicians, cooks, housekeepers, child-minders and gofers. But whether the volunteers are providing brains or brawn, clearly the satisfaction in vacations like these is very different from that of strolling the Champs-Elysées.

The volunteer task everybody associates most readily with retirement is caregiving. Whether in hospitals, nursing homes or private homes, seniors can be found taking care of all those who are forced into dependency, including one another. Among the American Association of Retired Persons' most successful efforts is its Long-Term Care Ombudsman Program, which works in nursing homes protecting the rights of frail elderly. But in effect, many baby boomers approaching retirement are already in training to take up society's caring imperative. They, especially the women, are being schooled in coping and kindness long before they themselves are ready to retire. When their retirement does arrive, many women of the baby-boom generation will have emerged from one of the 25 million American homes that have been taking care of an elderly relative.

The AARP estimates that three-quarters of the people looking after a sick or disabled family member in those households are women; others place the figure at 90 percent. Women have become the default caregivers of our society; they have been thrown into that role and forced to make the best of it. Theirs has been called the "sandwiched" life. No sooner do they finish raising their children than their ailing parents move in for care. As of the early nineties, the average age of women taking care of their parents was 57; more than one-third were over 65 and were destined to spend more of their lives "parenting" their parents than they had spent caring for their children.

Imagine for a moment women in their 50s and 60s saddled with this role for most of the rest of their lives. When anti-entitlements critics step forward presuming to speak for "our children," this is what makes their claim ring so hollow. Far from being helpless babes in arms, many of those "children" are themselves on the brink of retirement. And many more are already so burdened with home care that the last thing they want is to be "saved" from the "entitlements monster." As women demand help with this responsibility, our society will in a sense become more "feminized" in its values.

When enough people find themselves overloaded by prevailing home care arrangements, there will have to be changes. This is especially bound to be the case with assertive women who have been even remotely touched by feminist values. They could become a dominant electoral factor as politicians come to recognize where the votes are. As a matter of workaday practicality, the women's vote is a welfare-state vote. Even archconservatives have had to face up to the gender gap. In the name of family values, women demand more public money for schools, daycare, safe streets, food inspection. As if by cultural default in what has long been a "man's world," women care about these realities of everyday life and vote for them. Ideology will not answer their needs. Their vote is a clear cry for help.

Nursing homes are already an issue. The nursing home scandals of the eighties emerged as a bellwether issue in senior politics. The problem came to public awareness in 1985, when the media and Congressional investigators revealed the amount of elder abuse that was taking place in the cheap, unprofessional facilities many families were forced to use. The effort to improve long-term institutional care and make it affordable continues. When in 1992 budget-balancing conservatives in Congress began talking about measures to place a lien on the family home to pay for long-term care, the proposal was quickly dropped as unacceptable—and indeed morally reprehensible.

Full-time, full-scale home care, a burden that is already the blight of many women's lives, is bound to become just as urgent an issue as women find themselves sinking ever deeper into the harsh responsibilities that come with longevity. They will demand relief—and they will get it. With more money allocated for elder care, the caregiving sector of the economy will expand. In turn, caring will become a prominent occupation, even a profession. There are already young people specializing in elder care as gerontological doctors, nurses and counselors. It is not difficult to imagine this turning into a growth industry, a category of service employment that cannot be sent offshore or technologically eliminated. In the twenty-first century, geriatric care may take the place of high-tech as the unfolding frontier of opportunity.

> *The effort to improve long-term institutional care and make it affordable continues.*

Caregiving is not simply a family affair, nor can it be restricted to a profession. As medical science keeps more sick people alive, caring has turned into a spreading, grassroots feature of our society. It is already transforming neighborhoods, since it is neighbors who often have to intervene in the lives of the seriously ill. Much of this contact is casual and private—a simple understanding between friends that escapes public visibility—but the National Alliance for Caregiving estimates that more than 22 million households are now caring for neighbors as well as relatives. One federally funded effort called Gatekeepers enlists mail carriers and delivery drivers to learn about the neighborhoods they regularly visit, especially the shut-ins and the elderly who may need their help. They become part of a watchful mobile network of caregivers. Another rough measure: The National Federation of Interfaith Volunteer Caregivers, which trains and supports those who reach out to neighbors, has grown since the mid-eighties from twenty-five local chapters to more than 1,200. An important part of that increase has to do with the AIDS crisis in the gay community, many of whose members are taking on the role of traditional families for one another. That example has been appropriated for other forms of care, including elder care.

Increasingly, the basic units for elder care, as well as the care of the homebound sick, are the apartment complexes and condos where people find themselves living as age and illness descend upon them. With a few modest arrangements—a doorman to carry groceries, a visiting nurse, some taxi service, a few neighborhood children to run errands—people often prefer to "age in place." The AARP has discovered that our once-footloose baby-boom population has begun to put down roots. Almost half the country's older population has lived in the same place for more than twenty years. Researchers have come up with a quaint formal name for such an arrangement—NORCs: naturally occurring retirement communities. NORCs may become as characteristic of a longevous society as the suburbs were of the early lives of the boomers. But while suburbs isolated residents from one another and emphasized high consumption, NORCs and caring neighborhoods unite people and emphasize compassion.

When President Lyndon Johnson was formulating Medicare in the sixties, he also sought to create an Office of Aging at the Department of Health, Education and Welfare. The office would have overseen seniors serving in hospitals as medical aides. The American Medical Association thought this was a bad idea and vetoed it. The office was instead transformed into a little-known program called Serve and Enrich Retirement by Volunteer Experience (SERVE), which in turn led to the 1969 creation of the Retired and Senior Volunteer Program (RSVP).

RSVP is a little-publicized, vastly underfunded operation that continues to perform scores of vital services. In the mid-nineties, more than half a million seniors in RSVP projects served tens of thousands of sites across the country. They tutored in schools, assisted in clinics and courts, did some environmental watchdogging, participated in rehabilitation and telephone resource programs, served as companions for shut-in elders and took part in intergenerational projects. The contribution made by the Senior Companion Program is particularly valuable. In the mid-nineties, 12,000 volunteers helped more than 30,000 frail elders to live independently. With nursing home costs running as high as $35,000 a year, the estimated value of the companion service was $150 million.

Marc Freedman, writing in *The American Prospect*, regards RSVP as a "hidden triumph" of the Johnson Great Society. He calls this bare-bones beginning "the aging opportunity" and asks, Why not expand it in all directions as a comprehensive, well-funded national service program? He believes that with enough money behind it, RSVP—and similar state and local programs—could turn the retired into the "new trustees of civic life." The possibilities are vast. Retired teachers could become mentors, retired physicians could become medical counselors, retired lawyers could

> *NORCs [naturally occurring retirement communities] may become as characteristic of a longevous society as the suburbs were of the early lives of the boomers.*

become legal aides available for all the problems people have with employers, landlords and welfare and entitlement programs. There is a frontier of work and service waiting to be staked out by retired Americans.

Conservatives like to see volunteerism as an alternative to government. But the two could work in tandem, exchanging resources and inspiration. Government could empower the Third Sector—volunteer work outside the marketplace, either by individuals or through nonprofit organizations—often in very simple ways. For example, it could channel what is now welfare money through nonprofit and voluntary organizations to allow them to expand their work forces in the community. It could create a "shadow wage" that allows tax deductions for the value of the time one contributes to volunteer work.

Not all retired people are willing and able to work for nothing, of course. Several million Social Security recipients must scramble to supplement their meager government stipend. What they find are usually catch-as-catch-can part-time jobs at meager pay. It would clearly make far greater sense to pay retirees to work at something they know or to assume long-term caregiving responsibilities for members of their own generation. But by far the nearest, least bureaucratic way to achieve that goal is simply to give them higher Social Security payments so they will be free to volunteer.

> *There is a frontier of work and service waiting to be staked out by retired Americans.*

If the senior entitlements should become the model for a guaranteed annual income allied to a growing Third Sector, we would have the basis for a mature industrial economy in America. Such a compassionate economy would lend ballast to our otherwise turbulent marketplace. It would put retired skills to work. It would provide entry-level jobs for the otherwise unemployable young. It would put purchasing power in the hands of those who otherwise have nothing to spend. It would guarantee employment of last resort for all those who lose their jobs owing to global competition. As the pioneers of a robust Third Sector in the United States, the retiring boomers would be building a solid economic foundation for entitlements policy and the elder culture that rests upon it. Beyond protecting their own immediate interests in the entitlements debate, they would become the primary defenders of humane social values for all their more vulnerable fellow citizens, beginning with those who most clearly share the vulnerability of the elderly: the nation's children. It should be the highest priority on the senior political agenda to see the same right to a decent subsistence and full medical care granted to the young as to the old.

In one way or another, every budget-cutting attack on programs created to help the indigent, the disabled and the down and out impinges upon entitlements. Either the cost of entitlements is used to justify diminishing support to the needy, or continued funding of welfare programs for the needy is used to justify cutting entitlements. As part of the conservative backlash, Congressional leaders have been doing all they can to confuse "welfare" (temporary assistance to the unemployed and unemployable) with "welfare state" (Social Security and Medicare) in the public mind, two very differ-

---

It should be the highest priority on the senior political agenda to see the same right to a decent subsistence and full medical care granted to the young as to the old.

---

ent areas of policy that have different histories and goals. The aim of such deliberate obfuscation is to create the impression that seniors are living off "welfare" and should be ashamed to accept handouts. The very concept of "entitlement" is being called into question, as if to ask: Is anybody *entitled* to anything they did not earn in the marketplace?

In the seventies, mordant critics spoke of the baby boomers as the "me" generation, as if selfishness had previously been an unknown vice. When they leveled the charge, it was never clear what generation they had in mind as the appropriate ethical baseline. But if that accusation was ever true, the dynamics of the longevity revolution are bound to lay it to rest. Before they leave the stage of history, America's baby boomers, the first generation to face up to the challenge of creating an economics of permanence, may translate "me" into "we."

Ageing Workers[4]

A Full Life

ANONYMOUS
THE ECONOMIST, SEPTEMBER 4, 1999

Joe Clark is a happy man. Eighteen months ago, he might not have expected to be. After 21 years as an industrial engineer at a division of Harvard Industries in Tennessee, he found himself, when the plant shut down, out of a job at the age of 62.

"I tried retirement," he recalls. "But I was just piddling about the house. So I went to a job fair and left my resumé with several temporary-employment agencies." Within six weeks he was on the payroll of Manpower Technical. Now Manpower is employing him to look at ways to cut packaging costs for a car-parts firm. "I really look forward to coming to work."

Mr. Clark's new life is one that many older workers might covet. He is applying skills he has acquired over 40 years of working, but without the stress and responsibility of line management. He can take a day off whenever he needs one: that was part of the deal. He is earning about as much as he did in full-time work, but without the need to pay money into a pension scheme. And, when his wife retires in two years' time, he will be able to cut down to working six months a year, so they can spend more time together.

He is also a curiosity: he is in his early 60s and still at work. In the United States, only half the men aged between 60 and 64 are still in the labour force. That is more than Germany, where just over one-third still work—or France and the Netherlands, where the figure is less than one-fifth. Retirement, a concept that barely existed a century ago, now begins so early that men spend only half their lives in work [see chart 1 on p. 34].

Put early retirement together with the fall in fertility and the rise in life expectancy among the old, and a momentous change is occurring. Ahead lies a continued rise in the ranks of the retired—the "Florida effect," in the phrase of Peter Peterson, author of a recent book on the impact of ageing—and a decline in the population of working age [see chart 2 on p. 34]. In the 15 countries of the European Union, the population will not change between now and

---

2020—but the number aged between 25 and 50 will fall by an eighth, from 139m to 122m. In Britain, the fall will be 8%; in Germany, 11%; in Italy, 19%. In America, with its high immigration, that age group will continue to grow, but only by perhaps 3% over the whole period.

A contracting labour market is something none of today's employers has ever seen. Disturbing for the United States, it is even more worrying for Europe and Japan, where the fall in fertility has been sharper and immigration has been lower. "Populations in Europe are poised to plunge on a scale not seen since the Black Death in 1348," says Paul Wallace, author of another book on global ageing. "Poised" and "plunge" may put it a little strongly—even in Japan, population decline is unlikely before 2010—but the implications for countries and companies are certainly large.

Up to now, policymakers have tended to assume that the main effect of ageing will be on the affordability of pensions. In fact, the more dramatic effects will be on growth and living standards, as the world's most productive countries become its oldest. Last year, the OECD heroically tried to guess the consequences in the first half of the next century. Such forecasts, while bound to be wrong, at least suggest the scale and direction of changes. Moreover, demographic trends change slowly: the old of the next half-century have all been born already.

> *... there is no biological basis for a retirement age in the 60s.*

By 2040, guesses the OECD in a working paper published last year, the rise in the ratio of dependent old to working young may be reducing Japan's growth in living standards by three-quarters of a percentage point and Europe's and America's by half a point. The cumulative effect by mid-century could be to cut Japan's living standards by 23%, Europe's by 18% and America's by 10% below the level they might have reached otherwise.

The biggest driver of these cuts is demographic change. But most companies are also ill-prepared for a workforce of ageing baby-boomers. "Employers still have a mindset of getting people out the door at the earliest age," says Scott Morris of the Committee for Economic Development, an American think-tank which is about to publish a "wake-up call for employers, workers and government."

Employers who are likely to wake up first are those with the oldest workforces. In youthful America, some industrial firms have middle-aged workforces who will begin to retire in droves in the coming decade. The car companies are prime examples. At Ford, the average age of the 100,000 hourly workers is 44; at General Motors, it is 48.

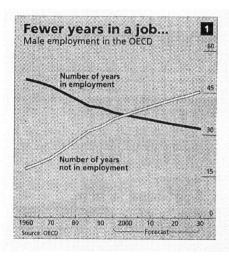

Fewer years in a job...
Male employment in the OECD

Number of years
in employment

Number of years
not in employment

1960 70 80 90 2000 10 20 30
Source: OECD   Forecast

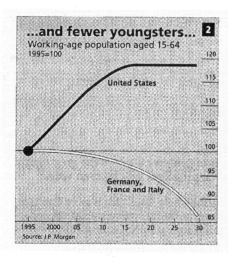

...and fewer youngsters...
Working-age population aged 15-64
1995=100

United States

Germany,
France and Italy

1995 2000 05 10 15 20 25 30
Source: J.P. Morgan

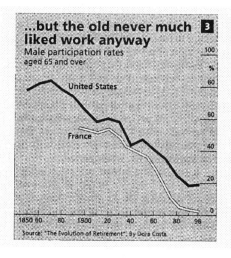

...but the old never much liked work anyway
Male participation rates
aged 65 and over

United States

France

1850 60 80 1900 20 40 60 80 96
Source: "The Evolution of Retirement". By Dora Costa

The car companies say that age diversity is wonderful and that they can recruit youngsters to take the places of retiring greyheads. But they also fret about this coming tidal wave of retirement: "We are concerned with losing skilled, seasoned people," says Megan Giles, at DaimlerChrysler. "We look at the next five years and know it's going to be a year-in-year-out problem."

The change in the balance of young and old is not easily reversible. What about early retirement? On the face of it, the rush to retire early is surprising. For one thing, the old seem healthier than ever before. A report by the OECD, "Maintaining Prosperity in an Ageing Society," suggests that disability is not generally a barrier to activity until people reach their mid-70s. Until people grow very old, differences in health *within* age groups are more important than differences *among* them. One implication: there is no biological basis for a retirement age in the 60s.

Not only are the old healthier than ever; they are growing healthier still. Research at Duke University in the United States has found that disability among the over 65s has been falling at an accelerating pace—the result, perhaps, of better education, nutrition, medicine, public health and pay. The babyboomers may do better yet: today's middle-aged have given up smoking, worry about their diet and go jogging at the weekend. Tedious, perhaps—but they will doubtless enjoy an even fitter third age than today's younger pensioners are doing.

They will, moreover, have less strenuous jobs: sitting at a desk rather than lugging bricks. Eugene Steuerle of the Urban Institute, an American thinktank, calculates that the share of American workers in physically demanding jobs has dropped from 20.3% in 1950 to 7.5% in 1996, with the fastest declines in the older age groups.

So why don't old folk stay in these cushier jobs? Part of the answer seems to be: because it makes little economic sense to do so. For a number of reasons, the benefits of retirement have risen, relative to the costs.

Many governments, especially in Europe, spent lavishly in the late 1970s and early 1980s to bribe older workers out of the job market, reasoning that retirement was less humiliating for the old than unemployment for the young. Early retirement is back in fashion again: in Germany, the government's Alliance for Jobs, a roundtable of ministers, employers and trade unions that aims to bring down unemployment, has discussed letting older workers draw their pensions early and switch to part-time work. The labour minister, Walter Riester, has floated plans to bring the retirement age down from 65 to 60. In France, the government is considering extending an early-retirement scheme it has agreed with the car industry.

Such schemes not only store up problems for the future. They also send a clear message to companies: unload the old. In countries with company pension schemes, that message is often reinforced by a surplus that allows them to buy out their older employees and so reduce their staff costs. The result, says Alan Walker of Sheffield University, who wrote a report on "Combating Age Barriers in Employment" for the European Foundation for the Improvement of Living and Working Conditions, has been to create "a culture of early retirement, where companies often think their older workers don't want to stay on."

Even in countries which have stopped deliberately promoting early retirement, governments—and companies—often unintentionally encourage early retirement, by imposing a heavy implicit tax on working for too many years.

Thus in some countries, it is illegal to work while drawing a pension. In others, workers can draw a pension only if they first leave their current job. Given the difficulty older workers have in finding work, that in effect condemns them to unemployment. Many countries withdraw some pension entitlement from working pensioners. In the United States, pensioners aged under 65 lose $1 for every $2 they earn over $9,600. Add in payroll taxes and income tax, and that is the equivalent of a marginal tax rate of up to 80%. As for workers who stay on the job, they rarely gain much in extra entitlements. That further boosts the implicit tax on work.

Company pension schemes have similar effects. One study of pension plans and employment records at several *Fortune* 500

companies found that the ages of retirement in those firms corre-
lated almost exactly with the financial incentives in their pension
plans, which generally encouraged retirement before 65. Indeed, the
impact of changes in such pension plans, for the workers covered by
them, seemed even stronger than the impact of reforming Social
Security.

While work has become less rewarding, leisure has become more
so. These days, the old have fun—and the money to enjoy it. Dora
Costa, an economist at MIT who last year published an important
study of retirement, argues that "retirement has become much more
attractive. Retired people are no longer usually living with their
children, and can move to low-cost places such as Florida." Television provides endless free entertainment; travel costs less than ever
before. In her book, she quotes one man who retired at 60 and
clearly loved every minute of it:

> My wife and I have completely changed our lifestyle since
> retirement. We live in a 31-foot Airstream trailer—spend
> seven months in winter in Melbourne, Florida, where we
> have every kind of activity. We dance and square-dance
> and party all winter. Then in summer we travel about—
> stop and spend some days with children and
> grandchildren and the rest of the time sightseeing from
> Canada through 48 states and Mexico. My goal in trying to
> retire early was to be able to do just this kind of thing
> before either my wife, who is older, or I become unable
> physically to do as we have been doing for six years now.

Not only are such delights less expensive than in the past; the old
are wealthier. Once, many were paupers. Now, in some countries,
they are better off than the working-aged population. Having lived
through half a century of growing prosperity to enjoy generous pensions, they have the public and private means to enjoy life.

Come back, we need you

What would it take to persuade older workers to stay in the job
market? The answer seems likely to emerge first in the United
States. There, the flight of older men from the job market seems to
have stopped since the mid-1980s. Indeed, a higher proportion of
men aged 62 or over are in the job market now than in 1985. Nobody
yet knows, however, whether the halt is permanent or merely a
pause.

The case for the pause is put by Ms. Costa. Early retirement, she
points out, is not just a recent trend, driven by taxes and benefits.
The employment rates of older men have been falling since 1880,
when fewer than 3% of Americans were over 64 but at least three

quarters of those were still toiling [see chart 3 on p. 34]. In the early years of this century, a small rise in pension entitlement relative to pay produced a large rise in retirement. As the century went by, the lure of a bigger pension dwindled. "If incomes continue to rise as economic growth progresses and if leisure-time activities continue to be relatively inexpensive and enticing, then the rise of retirement is unlikely to reverse."

Her view is challenged by Joseph Quinn, an economist at Boston College. He argues that a series of policy changes have removed some of the barriers that discouraged older men from working. Companies are prohibited by law from setting mandatory retirement ages. Congress has steadily increased the share of every dollar earned that a retired person can keep without losing Social Security entitlement and is raising the extra benefit entitlement that a worker can accumulate by delaying retirement. And in the private sector, the share of pensioned workers covered by defined-contribution pension plans, which are usually age-neutral, rose from 13% in 1975 to 42% in 1997.

But those, of course, are not the only changes that matter. In addition, the economy is booming. At Manpower, a giant temporary-employment agency, Sharon Canter, director of strategic information, says that 25-30% of the people placed are at least 50 years old. In America, some are over 80. "Labour is so short that our client companies are pleased to get qualified workers." Manpower scours churches and community groups for older people who might not have thought of returning to work, and boasts that more than a quarter of the 500,000 people it has trained in computer skills are "gold-collar" workers aged over 50.

Until the American boom stops fizzing, it may be impossible to be sure whether the change is permanent—or how far it will go. What is clear, however, is that the old are more likely to stay in the workforce if the kind of jobs on offer meet their needs—and those of prospective employers.

A Job for Life

Given the speed at which their workers are growing greyer, employers know surprisingly little about how productive they are. The general assumption is that the old are paid more in spite of, rather than because of, their extra productivity. That might partly explain why, when employers are under pressure to cut costs, they persuade the 55-year-olds to take early retirement. Earlier this year, Sun Life of Canada, an insurance company, announced that it was offering redundancy to all its British employees aged 50 or over "to bring in new blood."

In Japan, says Mariko Fujiwara, an industrial anthropologist who runs a thinktank for Hakuhodo, Japan's second-largest advertising agency, most companies are bringing down the retirement age from the traditional 57 to 50 or thereabouts—and in some cases, such as Nissan, to 45. More than perhaps anywhere else, pay in Japan is linked to seniority. Given that the percentage of workers who have spent more than 32 years with the same employer rose from 11% in 1980 to 42% by 1994, it is hardly surprising that seniority-based wage costs have become the most intractable item on corporate profit-and-loss accounts.

In Germany, Patrick Pohl, spokesman for Hoechst, expresses a widely held view: "The company is trying to lower the average age of the workforce. Perhaps the main reason for replacing older workers is that it makes it easier to 'defrost' the corporate culture. Older workers are less willing to try a new way of thinking. Younger workers are cheaper and more flexible." Some German firms are hampered from getting rid of older workers as quickly as they would like. At SGL Carbon, a graphite producer, the average age of workers has been going up not down. The reason, says the company's Ivo Lingnau, is not that SGL values older workers more. It is collective bargaining: the union agreement puts strict limits on the proportion of workers that may retire early.

Clearly, when older people do heavy physical work, their age may affect their productivity. But other skills may increase with age, including many that are crucial for good management, such as an ability to handle people diplomatically, to run a meeting or to spot a problem before it blows up. Peter Hicks, who co-ordinates OECD work on the policy implications of ageing, says that plenty of research suggests older people are paid more because they are worth more.

And the virtues of the young may be exaggerated. "The few companies that have kept on older workers find they have good judgment and their productivity is good," says Mr. Peterson. "Besides, their education standards are much better than those of today's young high-school graduates." Companies may say that older workers are not worth training, because they are reaching the end of their working lives: in fact, young people tend to switch jobs so frequently that they offer the worst returns on training. "The median age for employer-driven training is the late 40s and early 50s," says Mr. Hicks. "It goes mainly to managers."

Take away those seniority-based pay scales, and older workers may become a much more attractive employment proposition. But most companies (and many workers) are uncomfortable with the idea of reducing someone's pay in later life—although workers on piece-rates often earn less over time. So retaining the services of older workers may mean employing them in new ways.

One innovation, described in Mr. Walker's report on combating age barriers, was devised by IBM Belgium. Faced with the need to cut staff costs, and having decided to concentrate cuts on 55-60-year-olds, IBM set up a separate company called SkillTeam, which re-employed any of the early retired who wanted to go on working up to the age of 60. An employee who joined SkillTeam at the age of 55 on a five-year contract would work for 58% of his time, over the full period, for 88% of his last IBM salary. The company offered services to IBM, thus allowing it to retain access to some of the intellectual capital it would otherwise have lost.

... retaining the services of older workers may mean employing them in new ways.

The best way to tempt the old to go on working may be to build on such "bridge" jobs: part-time or temporary employment that creates a more gradual transition from full-time work to retirement. Mr. Quinn, who has studied the phenomenon, finds that, in the United States, nearly half of all men and women who had been in full-time jobs in middle age moved into such "bridge" jobs at the end of their working lives. In general, it is the best-paid and worst-paid who carry on working: "There are," he says, "two very different types of bridge job-holders—those who continue working because they have to and those who continue working because they want to, even though they could afford to retire."

If the job market grows more flexible, the old may find more jobs that suit them. Often, they will be self-employed. Sometimes, they may start their own businesses: a study by David Storey of Warwick University found that, in Britain, 70% of businesses started by people over 55 survived, compared with an average of only 19%. To coax the old back into the job market, work will not only have to pay. It will need to be more fun than touring the country in an Airstream trailer, or seeing the grandchildren, or playing golf. Only then will there be many more Joe Clarks.

The End of the Workday—II[5]

Discrimination against the Middle-aged Pervades the Workplace—at High Cost

By Margaret Morganroth Gullette
The Nation, January 5, 1998

Full-time work may soon become a privilege denied to middle-aged women and men, with 50 the end of the line even for the well educated. Most of us know someone who has lost a once-secure job at good wages with benefits, searched fruitlessly for the same kind of position and settled silently into subemployment. Few such people receive pensions, and most don't even qualify for unemployment. Those who find new jobs typically recover only a percentage of their former salaries. Although midlife subemployment—especially among white middle-class men—has been widely reported, its wider effects have not been fully explored. These days, according to some estimates, as many as a third of all workers are afraid of losing their jobs. For people at midlife, fear can reasonably verge on dread.

A large study in the eighties by the MacArthur Research Network on Successful Midlife Development revealed that 90 percent of white men between 45 and 49 were employed full time, but among those five years older, only 77 percent were—a surprising 14 percent drop. College-educated men suffered a drop of 9 percent. Since these data were gathered in 1987-88, the midlife work force has suffered from downsizing, capital flight, technological displacement and continuing real-income decline—which translate at the individual level into early "retirement," part-time "flexible" work without benefits, or unemployment. Between 1993 and 1995, during the "long economic recovery," 6 percent of all working women between 45 and 54 were displaced (left work involuntarily). This is a new discrimination: ageism directed at those in their middle years.

Americans expect our earnings to increase as we age into new responsibilities and social roles: as parents, teachers and coaches, moral authorities, political guides. Respect in the middle years partly depends on this rising curve, and midlife rewards are part of the American Dream—an unacknowledged hope for some, an unacknowledged entitlement for others. During the past thirty years, in

---

response to greater upward mobility, African-Americans, immigrants and their children, as well as white women, have also come to anticipate this result. "Seniority"—a word resonant with values from an older time—sums up unstated promises, psychological, social, economic, ethical and political. Discrimination against people in their middle years destroys this life-course dream. It foils the intention to provide education for kids (when the inability to pay for college creates desperate class divisions), help older children start out, save for retirement, support ailing parents. Family income should be highest when two generations are in the work force, but increasingly, the midlife generation is being forced down or out while the younger has yet to find its niche.

The "aging baby boomers," as the media slyly label them, have been promised great advantages for the midlife: positive aging, respect for older women, new choices. But none of this can come about without a high age-wage peak distributed democratically. America is far from that: Now it is mostly the very rich who see no decline before death. Only those in the remaining, mostly modest, seniority systems—unions, government, academe—see their earnings peak at retirement. Tenure is the model of lifetime security and age-wage increases over a person's entire working life—an ideal to be fought for and expanded to other groups and classes. (It's not an accident that all these institutions are under attack.) On average, men's incomes peak between 45 and 54, but this privilege, too, is available primarily to white men in the middle class. Already, college-educated men between 45 and 54 have seen their wages drop in constant dollars from $55,000 in 1972 to $41,900 in 1992. Women's incomes in general still peak a decade earlier than men's, between 35 and 44.

If the current trend of middle-ageism continues, the peaks will be lower and come sooner. More of the privileged will experience the midlife declines that the working class now suffers. This proletarianization of the life course would be a historical change of immense consequence. Without seniority, legal and/or customary, people aging into their middle years have no life chances. Research shows that in the working class, where wages peak earlier, people say they feel "old" at a younger age than those in the middle class do. ("You're only as old as you feel," the saying goes—but how you feel may depend a lot on your class.) Although the boomers are supposed to be getting richer as they turn 50, that may be another media distortion, promulgated just at the moment when more of them slide down the age-wage curve. And some writers are now chanting the delights of no longer working at 55. Sure, on what pension?

The costs of middle-ageism are high. If the current midlife generation does not resist for its own sake, we will permit this flattened, foreshortened system to pass on to our children. Without seniority, the first wage a young adult earns could be the highest one she or he will ever see. Although a rising age-wage system produces apparent life-course inequality—the young start out earning less than their elders—it's the most decent system in the long view. Young people need to understand that only the seniority system will help them in their turn. The generational warfare carried on by Pete Peterson and the Generation X groups fueled by the right wing has convinced some twenty-somethings that the *relative* affluence of the midlife generation is unfair. Such distortions can occur only in an economic culture actively crushing not only the practice of seniority but the value of the midlife. Although young people appear to benefit from this cult of youth, in the end they too will come to be considered old more quickly.

Young people need to understand that only the seniority system will help them in their turn.

Middle-ageism is useful to employers in business and government. It imputes losses of ability, slower reflexes and techno-retardation to justify downgrading of midlife employees. In an era when computers have phenomenal "memory," memory loss is represented as a particularly midlife problem.

Some midlife people withdraw from action, not-so-mysteriously turning into the grumpy caricatures we were taught to deride. If aging were the problem, how indeed could anyone resist it? A nation so demoralized is dangerous—likely to be mean-spirited to "losers" domestically, belligerent abroad. In all these ways the weakening of the midlife constitutes a midlife crisis for the nation. Shortsightedly driving wages to the bottom, the agents of these changes are blind or indifferent to their cultural effects. But they are not only forgoing the abilities of midlife individuals and damaging their lives; by tinkering with the life course, they are also changing what it means to Americans to be human.

Can 76 million boomers and the millions now over 50 join together to prevent these dire outcomes? This crisis could inspire unprecedented coalitions. Many of the solutions we already know, since European states have had two decades of experience with shedding midlife workers. The best European responses depend on the "work principle" rather than welfare, but allow respectable ways out of work-force participation for some people at midlife: lowering the age of Social Security benefits, especially for those who have worked in dangerous occupations or who are caring for elderly parents, and expanding disability programs. (In the United States, however, conservatives are threatening to raise the age at which Social Security benefits begin.) Full-employment policies would assure work for those who can do it at any age. This might mean a shorter work-week at steady pay, as the French are trying to achieve; or it might extend the concept of overtime to professionals. Full employment requires a livable minimum wage, expanded training programs, unemployment insurance and enforcement of midlife antidiscrimi-nation laws. These would eliminate the contrived scarcity that pits adult children against their parents for jobs and other goods.

But Americans also need to realize that "middle age" as we cur-rently live it is not an innocent fact of life. It is an ideological con-struct with psychological, social, economic and political   conse-quences. We need to see much more clearly how age is being manipulated (like race and gender) to divide the body politic. Age is a nice new devil, but instead of blaming it for the loss of hope and the crushing of dreams, we must see where the responsibility really belongs: on the global forces producing middle-ageism.

Hunger in America[6]

Five million elderly Americans have no food, or worry about getting enough to eat

BY TRUDY LIEBERMAN
THE NATION, MARCH 30, 1998

Randall Mueck's job at San Francisco's meal clearinghouse is to decide who will get food and who will wait. In mid-January, 411 of the city's homebound elderly were on Mueck's waiting list, 100 more than a few months earlier. All qualify for a hot, home-delivered meal under the federal Older Americans Act, but there isn't enough money to feed everyone.

Seniors who move up the fastest are those in the custody of adult protective services, the dying and the very old. Twenty-five percent of the people asking for food are over 90. "I try to think of all 411 and fit someone in accordingly," Mueck explains. "Age is going to bump somebody way up."

That means Audrey Baker, 79, must wait. When she asked for help last September, Mueck assigned her 750 points out of the 900 or so she needed to qualify for a meal. In January, her score had reached 877. (Each day on the list adds a point.) Baker, a thin woman, is blind, falls a lot and is on the mend from a broken back. She also has hypertension and diabetes.

"I've outlived everybody else in my family," Baker says. "I don't have any friends." Her only help is an aide who comes for two hours on Fridays. Like many seniors, Baker is vague about what she eats. "It's whatever I can afford," she says. What will she eat this week? "I'll eat all right, but I don't know exactly what." Tonight it's an apple and some nuts.

Food isn't far from her mind, though. On the table beside the armchair in her tiny living room is a copy of the food magazine *Cooking Light*, in braille. "She's clearly struggling," says Frank Mitchell, a social worker with San Francisco's Meals on Wheels program. "How do you say, 'I know you're hungry. We'll serve you in three months'?"

But that's the reality all across the country. Thousands of elderly men and women too infirm to cook or even see the flames of the stove are put on ration lists for food in the most bountiful country in the world. A 1993 study by the Urban Institute found that some 5 million elderly have no food in the house, or worry about getting enough to eat. They experience what the social service business calls "food insecurity." In Miami alone, 2,000 people are waiting. Says John Stokesberry, executive director of Miami's Alliance for Aging, "By the time we clean up the waiting list, some will be dead." Another study, done for the federal Administration on Aging, looked at food programs during the 1993-95 period and found that 41 percent of the country's 4,000 providers of home-delivered meals to the elderly had waiting lists. Malnutrition among the elderly is commonplace: Researchers at Florida International University estimate that 63 percent of all older people are at moderate or high nutritional risk. Some 88 percent of those receiving home-delivered meals are at similar risk, according to a study by Mathematica Policy Research.

In the face of shifting demographics, the picture isn't likely to improve. The number of people 60 and older has increased from 31 million in 1973 to 44 million today. And the number of the oldest old, those over 85 for whom assistance with meals is crucial, is growing even faster: Almost 1.5 million people were over 85 in 1970; in 2000, their number will exceed 4 million.

The homebound elderly are largely invisible. They aren't glamorous, and giving them food is not at the cutting edge of philanthropy. They are the antithesis of the "greedy geezer" who has come to represent all of the elderly in the public mind. They have no lobbyists—the interests of senior organizations lie elsewhere. Politicians neglect them; they don't vote or make campaign contributions. Often their children have moved far from home, leaving them without caregivers, a dilemma more keenly felt by women, who usually live longer than men. In 1970, 56 percent of the elderly over age 75 lived alone; by 1995, 76 percent were living by themselves.

For many, there are no meal lists to get on. In Big Springs, a speck on the Nebraska prairie, 134 of the town's 495 residents are eligible for a meal. But there's no money to start a food program. Vic Walker, director of the Aging Office of Western Nebraska, doesn't even have enough money to feed those living outside the city limits of Scottsbluff, the largest town in the area. One man living on a ranch three miles over the line "needed a meal so desperately," recalls Irma Walter, Walker's case manager. "He was so debilitated, but there was no access to food."

The Federal Commitment

More than thirty years ago, in 1965, Congress recognized the lengthening life span and the infirmities that come with it, and enacted the Older Americans Act to help seniors live out their last days at home with essential support: transportation, household help and personal care. The act is not a welfare program; anyone over age 60 is eligible for services if there's room.

In his 1972 budget message, President Nixon noted that "a new commitment to the aging is long overdue," and two nutrition programs were added that year: centralized, or congregate, meal sites—now numbering about 16,000—where seniors could eat a hot lunch and socialize; and a delivery service to send a hot meal to the homebound elderly. Meals prepared by a cadre of local churches, social service agencies and nonprofit organizations, many with similar names, were meant to reach mobile seniors and the homebound in every nook and cranny of America.

The food programs were supposed to promote "better health" among the older population "through improved nutrition" and offer

---

Most Americans eat three meals each day, or 1,095 meals a year. The elderly receiving home-delivered meals get only 250.

"older Americans an opportunity to live their remaining years in dignity." Nixon pledged that the federal commitment would "help make the last days of our older Americans their best days."

At the beginning, Nixon tried to make good on that promise. When the Office of Management and Budget thought the initial funding should be $40 million and Nixon's adviser on aging, Arthur Flemming, suggested $60 million, Nixon upped the amount to $100 million. Throughout the seventies the funding kept pace with need. After that, however, it did not. Adjusting for inflation, per capita appropriations for all Older Americans Act programs in 1995 should have been $39. Actual per capita funding was only $19. Although total annual spending for all services has gone from $200 million in 1973 to $865 million today, that money not only hasn't kept up with inflation but it also hasn't kept up with the number of people who need help. The 1995 federal appropriations were down by about 50 percent relative to what the government spent in 1973. Money spent for the two food programs has shrunk by a similar amount.

Though payment is not mandatory, three-quarters of the elderly who get a home-delivered meal and almost everyone who eats at the congregate sites contributes, sometimes as little as 50 cents, toward the roughly $5.30 it costs to provide a meal. Half of those receiving home-delivered meals and about one-third of participants eating at congregate meal sites have annual incomes of less than $7,900. "Those least able to pay won't eat unless they put something in," says Larry Ross, the chief fiscal officer for San Francisco's Commission on the Aging.

One Meal A Day

Most Americans eat three meals each day, or 1,095 meals a year. The elderly receiving home-delivered meals get only 250. Only 4 percent of food providers routinely offer more than one meal a day, five days a week, and few offer weekend meals. In San Francisco, 765 people lucky enough to receive their food from Meals on Wheels, one of the city's nine providers, get two meals seven days a week. The rest of the city's 1,660 food recipients get only one. If the city's Commission on the Aging paid for two meals per person, as many as 400 people now served would not get any meal. The trade-off is constant and stark: Do more people get fewer meals or do fewer people get more meals?

The Salvation Army, which serves the meals in San Francisco's Tenderloin district, resolves the question in favor of the former, but there is pain whichever way it's answered. Richard Bertolovzi lives in an S.R.O. He is a skinny, bearded man with greasy hair, missing front teeth and one red eye that looks infected. "You don't deliver tomorrow, do you?" "Bert" asks the young woman delivering his noon meal of fish, coleslaw, fruit cocktail, clam chowder, corn bread, and milk. A curtain of disappointment falls over his face, and he looks away in disgust. "I'm hungry," he says. "I can eat anything. I have a loaf of bread, that's all. That's all I got. And I got some instant coffee." The Salvation Army is able to offer him only a can of Ensure, a nutritional drink, to get through the weekend.

The Limits of Philanthropy

Food providers have always had to look for donations to support their programs. Now they have to look even harder. "We're competing with more folks than ever," says Mary Podrabsky, president of the National Association of Nutrition and Aging Services Programs. The conventional wisdom these days is that philanthropy should do more and government as little as possible—or, as Heritage Foundation senior fellow Dan Mitchell puts it, "If it's worth doing, the private sector can do it."

When it comes to feeding the elderly, private-sector funding works a little bit in a few places, not at all in most others. San Francisco Meals on Wheels was able to raise $214,000 last year thanks in part to benefit dinners cooked by the city's top chefs. Its New York counterpart raised $8 million last year from direct-mail campaigns, social events, grants and corporate contributions to provide some weekend meals and to whittle down the city's waiting list, although some 700 people are still in the queue. This past November, New York Citymeals-on-Wheels fundraiser extraordinaire Marcia Stein raised $675,000 throwing a women's power luncheon at the Rainbow Room. Guests including Brooke Astor, Diane Sawyer and Lena Horne plunked down a minimum of $250 to dine on vegetable terrine and risotto with white truffles.

Towns like Ramona, California, population 30,000, high in the hills northeast of San Diego, have no such benefactors.

In the new world of corporate giving, charity is often tied to the bottom line.

Chuck Hunt, board president of the town's senior center, tells how he placed ads in the *Ramona Sentinel* and *North County Times* asking 1,000 people to pledge $100 or 2,000 people to give $50. He collected exactly $1,600—twelve people gave $100 and got on the center's "gold honor roll"; eight donated $50 for a place on the "silver honor roll." Hunt also wrote to Allied Signal Aerospace, where he had worked for twenty-six years, asking for $25,000 to pay down overdue food bills and repairs on the vans that deliver meals. He says he felt "let down" when his old employer said no.

Raising private money in places like Ramona or Big Springs, or even San Diego, is not easy. There are few large corporations and foundations to tap, and if there are any, they have little interest in feeding the elderly. "If you flat-out ask people for food for seniors, you don't get much of a response," says Daniel Laver, director of the Area Agency on Aging in San Diego. "Private foundations are looking at cutting-edge programs—new and innovative. Basic human needs programs are not as sexy."

In the new world of corporate giving, charity is often tied to the bottom line. During the holidays Kraft offered 600 meal providers $100 each if they placed a story about a Kraft promotion in their local media. Kraft said it would donate 25 cents to meal programs for each special coupon redeemed. To get the $100, however, providers had to submit press clippings showing they had fulfilled the deal's P.R. requirements. If they did, the $100 donation bought about twenty meals.

Such corporate "generosity" doesn't insure that seniors have enough to eat, nor can it build the necessary infrastructure of senior centers and food preparation sites; only adequate, continuing federal appropriations can do that. Says Bob Tisch, New York City-meals-on-Wheels board president, feeding the elderly "is the government's responsibility."

State and Local Aid

States must contribute at least 15 percent of the total cost of the two federal meal programs. Some states go beyond that. Pennsylvania, for instance, contributes its lottery proceeds to services for the elderly. Local governments sometimes kick in money, and where they do, those funds help keep the food programs afloat. County funds including a dedicated portion of San Francisco's parking tax make up about 38 percent of the budget for home-delivered meals. The City of New York contributes 55 percent of the food-program budget. Voters in Cincinnati have twice approved a property-tax levy to support a variety of services for the elderly, most recently last fall by a margin of 65 percent to 35 percent. Eighty-three percent of the Council on Aging's $4.1 million budget for home-delivered meals is funded by the tax levy. "It's a myth that people don't want to help their elderly," says Bob Logan, director of the council, the agency serving the Cincinnati area. He says the levy "was overwhelmingly supported by the young, the old, Republicans, Democrats, minorities and non-minorities." But even a generous stream of local money can't stop waiting lists from mounting: In Cincinnati, local money just means those on the lists don't have to wait as long.

Furthermore, food programs in some localities are in jeopardy because of diminishing local tax revenues. Take, for instance, Saunders County in eastern Nebraska, a suburb of nearby Omaha. In the past few years the county has contributed around $68,000 a year for both congregate and home-delivered meals. Still, that money is inadequate, forcing some communities to serve the elderly only two or three days a week. (The law allows a program to provide food fewer than five days a week in rural areas.)

Service could be slashed even further, a result of reduced inheritance taxes, which have funded food programs for the elderly, and the state legislature's recent imposition of a limit on local property tax levies. "Some services are going to be cut or slimmed back," says Patti Lindgren, the County Clerk. "The ones that will be are those optional to the county, like senior services."

Penny-Wise and Pound-Foolish

The United States has no national policy on aging. Instead, an unwritten policy directs resources to the most expensive care in the last places the elderly stay—hospitals and nursing homes. When malnourished seniors go to the hospital, they may end up staying longer and costing more money. The Massachusetts Dietetic Association estimates that for every $1 spent on nutrition programs, $3.25 is saved in hospital costs. A study in Little Rock compared two groups of hospitalized seniors who were the same age and had the same diagnosis. One group had received home-delivered meals; the other group had not. Patients who got food stayed in the hospital half as long as those who didn't. Ronni Chernoff, associate director of geriatric research at the V.A. hospital in Little Rock, who supervised the research, figured that the cost of eight extra days in the hospital—some $4,800 at Little Rock rates—was the equivalent of providing someone with a meal a day for two and a half years.

Despite the compelling statistics, no one in Congress seems willing to champion the cause of meals for the elderly.

An acute episode such as breaking a bone, healing a surgical incision or the flu makes demands that a poorly nourished body cannot accommodate. "The people I'm not serving but know in my heart of hearts I should are those just coming out of the hospital," says Gail Robillard, a nutritionist with the Jefferson Council on Aging in Metairie, Louisiana. Without such assistance, they often go back to the hospital, a vicious cycle that Robillard believes can be prevented with good nutrition. Medicare's home health care benefit covers the services of nurses, aides and a variety of therapies, but not food.

Without food, the elderly also go to nursing homes prematurely, adding to what is already a huge national expense. The United States spends about $80 billion a year on nursing-home care, nearly half paid by taxpayers through Medicaid. A year in a nursing home averages around $40,000; a year's worth of meals, $1,325.

Needed: A Champion

Despite the compelling statistics, no one in Congress seems willing to champion the cause of meals for the elderly. The closest these days is New York Senator Alfonse D'Amato, who pushed through a 3.5 percent increase in funds for congregate and home-delivered meals last year. In fact, says one Senate staffer, "there has been a general push to cut back on Older Americans Act appropriations for many years." Money from the Department of Agriculture, which also contributes to the programs, has been cut from about $150 million to $140 million, further limiting the number of meals providers can serve. A House staffer explains: "No one speaks ill of the program. On the other hand, no one gets excited about it." Lack of enthusiasm makes it an easy target to cut or ignore.

"The Older Americans Act has suffered because it is such a feel-good, sound-good act it doesn't translate into tangible things anyone can look at and champion so it gets the necessary increases," says Bob Blancato, director of the 1995 White House Conference on Aging. Food competes in the same spending bill with the National Institutes of Health, Head Start and bilingual education, more glamorous activities that are easier for members of Congress to embrace. Last year the N.I.H. got a $900 million increase, boosting its budget to more than $13 billion. This year the President has proposed another $1.1 billion. "There's a lot of exciting scientific stuff happening," says a House staffer. "Everybody knows someone who's sick, and that always gets people's interest." Sickness caused by hunger doesn't have the same cachet. Head Start and bilingual education have also fared better, thanks largely to the Clintons. Indeed, last year bilingual education got a 25 percent increase, one of the largest in the entire federal budget.

The President's budget calls for no increase in money for food programs for the elderly this year, although some fifty members of the House recently signed a letter to Clinton urging such an increase. One of those who signed is Frank LoBiondo, a New Jersey Republican who has also circulated a letter of his own asking his colleagues to oppose the President's spending freeze. "It's difficult when the President didn't recognize the importance [of the programs] in his budget," he says.

In the end, it will come down to a question of priorities, especially those of Representative Bob Livingston, a Republican from Metairie who chairs the House Appropriations Committee. Meanwhile, the nutrition programs in his district struggle; some people wait as long as thirteen months for a meal. Gail Robillard says she, too, is "prioritizing on top of prioritizing," trying to allocate food to the neediest. "Livingston says he's interested in the elderly, but nothing specific ever comes from him," she says.

Ask what they eat and seniors say they manage, putting the best face on the most dehumanizing of predicaments. It's too demeaning to say otherwise. Confessing hunger is an admission that you can't provide for your most basic need. Pressed for what they really eat, seniors are apt to say tea and toast, cereal, cookies, a sandwich of peanut butter or baloney, even scraps foraged from the garbage.

"I'm not proud to say we lived out of dumpsters," says 74-year-old Helen McCleery, whose disabled son scoured garbage bins before

McCleery got on the San Diego meal program. "We were eating whatever my son found—mostly vegetables. We washed the vegetables, sprayed them with Lysol and washed them again." They didn't touch meat, McCleery said; they were too afraid of E. coli and salmonella. Macular degeneration has taken her sight, and she is diabetic. She knows she wasn't eating right, but she and her son were living on $700 a month; their rent of $635 left little for food.

Unless there's renewed federal commitment to the elderly, their story will be repeated. It's the responsibility of everyone, says Michel Roux, president of Carillon Importers and board member of New York Citymeals-on-Wheels, "to think of these people as their parents."

II. Baby Boomers and the "New Aging"

Editor's Introduction

The baby boom generation comprises those born between 1946 and 1964, a period during which economic prosperity in the U.S. in the wake of World War II helped fuel unprecedented annual birthrates. At approximately 80 million people, the size of this generation alone gives it an enormous influence on American society. As Mary Pipher writes in *Another Country*, baby boomers "are the pig in the python, the big demographic bulge that has moved across the last half of our century. What happens to us happens to millions of people at once." It is arguable that the topic of aging began to receive more attention during the past several decades as boomers began to confront the aging of their parents. In 1996, the oldest boomers themselves turned 50 and thus began contributing toward an upward shift in the average age of Americans that had already been occurring throughout the 20th century. Some experts feel the maturing of this group, many of whom came of age in the 1960s and were regarded as the quintessential youth generation, will change our views about what it means to grow old. Baby boomers, by most accounts, bring to the aging process a firm conviction that they will be able to maintain a high degree of youthfulness—in their health, appearances, energy and activity levels, and outlooks on life—and many doctors and others contend they are right. However, some people question the lengths to which boomers are willing to go in order to delay what many believe to be the natural and inevitable effects of aging. By striving to stay young, they contend, boomers are cheating themselves of the full experience of their later years.

Much media attention has been devoted to recent scientific research that promises to extend the human life span and even turn back the clock. In addition to the enormous advances that have been made in fighting such age-related diseases as heart disease and Alzheimer's, newer research aims to uncover the biological processes involved in normal aging. Still other, often controversial research has spawned the new field of anti-aging medicine. In "Live A Lot Longer" (*Fortune*), David Stipp gives an overview of major findings related to the identification of genes that control the aging process, discoveries that often provide clues to the evolutionary reasons human beings age the way we do.

In "The Sky's the Limit" (*Los Angeles Times*), Bettijane Levine presents a few examples of highly active seniors, whose ranks are growing nationwide. These 70-and 80-somethings hike, ski, and skydive and have no intention of cutting back as they continue to age. Contrary to popular belief that says elderly people are primarily frail and vulnerable, doctors and experts maintain there is nothing stopping older people from engaging in vigorous activities, providing they are in good health. Research such as that conducted by John D. Rowe and Robert L. Kahn as part of the MacArthur Foundation Study of aging has shown that deterioration is a result of disease or poor habits, rather than an inevitable part of aging. (A chapter of Rowe and Kahn's highly regarded book, *Successful Aging*, is included in Section IV of this volume.) Gerontologist Robert N. Butler and others predict that the trend towards seniors being more active will continue to rise, as more and more baby boomers enter this stage in life.

Levine also quotes Butler as stating that social stigma is a major reason more seniors aren't pursuing such vigorous activities. Older people skydiving, for example, is so contrary to many Americans' preconceptions about aging that younger people are often disapproving. It is in part the stigma attached to age, and society's presumptions about older people, that have prompted increasing numbers of Americans to undergo plastic surgery in recent years. According to Sharon Walsh in "Baby Boom's New Wrinkle: A Rush to Cosmetic Surgery" (*Washington Post*), many who undergo cosmetic surgery are motivated by their desire, for both personal and professional reasons, to avoid being perceived as old.

In response to the new paradigm of aging, in which living longer and looking and feeling as young as possible are held by many to be paramount, there are a few who contend that what we really need is to accept old age as different from other stages in life. In "Let's Hear It For Decrepitude" (*New York Times*), Melvin Maddocks writes of the "subtle cruelty" of exhorting seniors to stay youthful. Hila Colman presents a likeminded view in her commentary "Just Desserts," published in the *New York Times Magazine's* "Lives" column. Like Maddocks, Colman writes of her wish that her old age be different from her youth, and revels in her newfound leisure time, likening it to dessert after the full meal of her previous years. She writes, "This is my time to enjoy the quietness of just being, of stopping to look and feel and think, of indulging myself. Time for myself at last."

Live a Lot Longer [1]

By David Stipp
Fortune, July 5, 1999

Chin up, fellow boomers, aging has its compensations. Our fingernails are growing slower, so we don't need to clip them as often. Our sweat glands are waning, so we have less body odor to worry about.

There's probably more, but I forget.

Oh, well, the debit side is more interesting anyway. It starts around age 25, when the ability to detect odors begins to go. Lung power and brain size peak about then and head south. General shrinkage sets in around 35, after which height diminishes and inexorable muscle degeneration begins. After 40 the skin begins losing its memory: Pinch the back of your hand hard at 45, and it smooths out in two seconds; by 65 it generally takes 20 seconds. After 50 our tissues start drying out, one reason weight usually drops after 55. Erotic daydreams, closely linked to sexual activity, dwindle and typically fade out around 65. The nose and ears elongate.

All this suggests why gerontology, the study of aging, is the true dismal science—not so much because the subject is a downer but because it encompasses the most bewildering hodgepodge of data in all of medicine. Our biological clocks tick at wildly different rates, a variability that has defeated gerontologists' quest for reliable "biomarkers" of aging. So even if there were a drug that slowed aging, there would be no practical way to prove it works—establishing that people who took it live longer would take decades. That's a major reason the drug industry has left the anti-aging business to quacks.

In fact, gerontology has long been a stagnant backwater tainted by snake oil, where baffled researchers grow old fishing up miscellany and piecing it into rickety hypotheses that sink soon after they're floated. By one count, more than 300 theories of aging have gone down with hardly a trace. Many scientists believe the aging process is sheer anarchy loosed upon the body, too complex to analyze, hence not worth the effort.

---

1. Article by David Stipp from *Fortune*, July 5, 1999. Copyright © 1999 *Fortune*. Reprinted with permission.

But quite unexpectedly, a range of new findings is snapping into focus the prospect of a radically new science of aging—one that points toward the possibility of lengthening human life span by the relatively simple manipulation of a small number of genes. If the new science pans out, almost everything will change, especially the meaning of "old." The population might soar. We would have to extend our working lives lest our nest eggs get used up too soon. Millions of parents might live on as their children reached ripe old ages—the two generations would jointly explore a vast temporal frontier opened at the far end of the human life span.

If you put together recent findings and stand back, you can already descry the engine of these changes: the first robust, big-picture theory on aging supported by a great diversity of data. Its core idea is that a wide array of creatures, from fruit flies to British aristocrats, possess a kind of life-span rheostat embedded in their genes. This genetic rheostat probably evolved so that animals, including humans, could adjust to their circumstances by applying the body's inner resources either to reproducing fast or to guarding their cells against the ravages of time. Certain stimuli, such as caloric restriction, can twirl the rheostat to cell-maintaining "hibernation mode"—it pays to hunker down and put reproduction on hold when food is scarce.

Importantly, several recent studies—including ones on centenarians and on a clan of fearless opossums on an island off the Georgia coast—suggest that a small number of genes, perhaps fewer than ten, governs the rheostat in mammals. If true, that's the best news of all: Therapeutically tweaking fewer than a dozen genes seems a tractable problem, unlike trying to address bodywide anarchy.

Now the hunt is on for the rheostat genes, whose discovery would pave the way for anti-aging drugs. The quest's implications dwarf those of any other line of medical research, notes David Harrison, who studies long-lived mice at Jackson Laboratory in Bar Harbor, Me. Since aging is by far the biggest risk factor for almost every major disease in the developed world, drugs that brake it would curb a myriad of scourges at one fell swoop. When the Reaper finally got us, he'd be hopping mad—we'd have cheated him both by living longer and by spending a larger proportion of our lives in good health.

All this hinges on big ifs. Some gerontologists, prominently the University of Washington's George M. Martin, argue that time's toll involves thousands of genes—he dismisses talk of anti-aging therapies coming anytime soon as "simplificationist" dreaming.

Therapies to extend our lives to 150 aren't bubbling up in the lab yet, contrary to recent effusions of pop gerontology in the media. But "the gloom is gone" in gerontology, declares Steven Austad, a University of Idaho zoologist who studies aging. If he and other guarded optimists are right, the field is about where bacteriology was in the 1870s, when a flurry of discoveries linking germs to diseases paved the way for the antibiotic revolution—and this century's huge upswing in life expectancy.

New talent and money are flowing in. When biologist Gary Ruvkun realized a few years ago that his work had major implications for gerontology, he initially was nonplussed. "I thought, 'Oh, God, now I'm in aging research—your IQ halves every year you're in it,'" says Ruvkun, who studies genetics in tiny worms called nematodes at Boston's Massachusetts General Hospital. Now the National Institute on Aging and a foundation set up by Larry Ellison, Oracle's billionaire CEO, have awarded him grants to study genes that make some nematodes live three times longer than normal. "This field looks like it's going somewhere quickly," Ruvkun says.

But "the gloom is gone" in gerontology, declares Steven Austad, a University of Idaho zoologist who studies aging.

More than a dozen gene mutations have been discovered over the past decade that dramatically extend the life spans of certain animals, including worms, flies, and mice—a sign there's more genetic rhyme and reason to aging than previously thought. Buttressing that view are studies on the Olympic athletes of aging, human centenarians, whose numbers have risen enough in recent years to reveal that extreme longevity runs in families, suggesting a strong genetic influence on aging. Other studies are probing genes that are activated in slow-aging animals on low-calorie diets—caloric restriction, the only well-established life extender, can keep a mouse lively for a span roughly equal to 150 human years.

Researchers have inserted genes in fruit flies that extend their lives, on average, by about 50%. Clues abound about where to look for life-span-rheostat genes in higher animals. Some of the genes appear to retard growth. Thus scientists have scoured the world for undersized mice and scanned the medical literature for cases of "leprechaunism" caused by rare human mutations. Toy dogs like Chihuahuas are getting a close look too.

Perhaps the hottest leads are the ones coming from worms. Ruvkun showed in 1997 that a life-extending gene in nematodes bears a striking resemblance to a human gene involved in regulating blood sugar—a finding that fits with the idea of life-span rheostats geared to the availability of food. It also suggests that the "hibernation response" is one of evolution's most ancient inventions. Genes underlying it may have been conserved, as biologists say, through the eons, hence may be widely shared across species.

If so, says University of Michigan gerontologist Richard A. Miller, a leading proponent of the rheostat idea, then life-extending genes "may well be hidden in our fields, orchards, kennels, and perhaps even among our colleagues."

Like most big ideas, the rheostat one isn't all that novel in some respects. The notion of a tradeoff between reproducing and long life was around long before the era of exhausted working couples. One indicator of that is the tendency of long-lived animals, such as humans, to start reproducing later and have fewer offspring than short-lived creatures, such as rabbits. Some animals, like salmon, age at light speed after reproductive bursts. This pattern makes sense in light of a gloomy Darwinian theorem: Our genes are designed by evolution to keep us going strong only until we reproduce. Soon after the peak reproductive years, genes that protect us from aging start losing their beneficent force. Then things get random, and our bodies wear out as insults such as "free radicals," the notorious chemical cousins of oxygen that can clobber DNA and other cellular molecules, take their toll.

> *... life-extending genes "may well be hidden in our fields, orchards, kennels, and perhaps even among our colleagues."*
> —gerontologist Richard A. Miller

This theorem, one of few ideas about aging with staying power, was detailed in 1952 by immunologist Peter Brian Medawar. The logic: Consider two gene mutations that might have arisen separately in a couple of our Stone Age forerunners. One promotes agility during youth; the other retards muscle deterioration after 40. Say the bearers of these two genetic gifts, at age 10, find themselves facing a saber-toothed tiger. The one with the agility gene might leap clear, enabling him to live long enough to pass on his gene, which likely would be spread by his progeny and become a standard fixture in the genome. The one with the other mutation probably wouldn't get to pass it along—aging gracefully didn't matter during the time evolution was sculpting our genomes, when disease, accidents, and predators limited life span to about 30.

The ominously named "disposable soma" hypothesis, championed by British researcher Thomas B. L. Kirkwood, added a twist to Medawar's theory: It brought to the forefront the "cost" of making babies. Kirkwood posits that the more energy we invest in reproduction, the less we can expend on metabolic systems that slow aging. One such system includes antioxidant enzymes that mop up the free radicals our cells churn out as they burn sugar to produce energy. People who grow fast and reach puberty early, enabling speedy reproduction, may be genetically geared to put fewer inner resources into making antioxidants, hence age faster, than those who aren't built for reproductive speed. Our selfish genes are willing to make such tradeoffs since they effectively regard our bodies as disposable egg cartons, no longer necessary once the genes have sprung forth to the next generation of throwaway bodies, or "somas."

This theory got a big boost in 1984 when Michael Rose, a researcher at the University of California at Irvine, reported a simple experiment: By selectively breeding normal fruit flies that tended to reproduce unusually late in life, he generated flies of increasing longevity—in effect, he forced the insects to trade early fertility for slower aging. Eventually he got ones that lived nearly twice as long as their ancestors.

Last year Kirkwood reported a similar finding in humans, based on genealogical records on British aristocrats born between 740 and 1875. The study shows that among women who reached at least age 60, those who had many children early in life tended to die younger than those who had fewer kids, relatively late. A similar pattern was found among the men.

Given all this, you'd think the mystery of aging had a tidy solution: After we pass our reproductive primes, our genes simply step back and let us get trashed by free radicals and other random damage. But some things don't fit. One is emerging data that conflict with the Danish twin study, which many gerontologists look to like a lighthouse in the murk. Published in 1993, it's regarded as having established that environmental factors, not genes, are what predominantly influence longevity—just as you'd expect if genes' life-preserving power wanes a few years after puberty.

Twins make good subjects for determining this issue—if genes dominate, then identical twins, who are genetic duplicates, should have about the same life spans. But after examining data on twins born in Denmark between 1870 and 1888, researchers estimated that genes account for only about 30% of longevity. That implies environmental factors are the primary influence.

The twin data also imply that only about one in 400 centenarians has a centenarian sibling. That would make sense if the effect of environment dominates, because by age 100, the influence of the twins' shared genes on aging is overwhelmed by life's wear and tear. Thus centenarian siblings should be as rare as a brother and sister who separately win millions in the state lottery.

But new studies on centenarians are turning up more hyper-old siblings than the Danish findings predict. Catherine McCaig, a 103-year-old subject in the New England Centenarian Study at Harvard Medical School, is a member of one of these surprising "sibships." She lives in Marshfield, Mass., near her 94-year-old sister Winifred Whynot and, until recently, their brother Nat, who died at 94. A truly astonishing sibship found by the Harvard team included four siblings who lived past 100 and a 97-year-old sister; the siblings also had seven centenarian cousins. The odds of such cases occurring by chance, rather than by inherited genes, are vanishingly small, notes Thomas Perls, the study's director.

Perls argues that the Danish twins may have yielded misleading results because only a few of them reached their 80s and none lived past 90. Thus they couldn't reveal the effects of longevity-enabling genes that are manifested in centenarians—just as studying the running speeds of wild horses wouldn't necessarily reveal how thoroughbreds can inherit the wind.

Another sign of longevity genes' existence is the fact that there is no centenarian lifestyle—researchers studying the hyper-old have repeatedly failed to find commonalities in diet or exercise, or any other environmental factor, that could explain their longevity. Some centenarians say they've eaten very little red meat through their lives, while others ate it every day, notes Perls. One of his subjects had a daily breakfast of three eggs and bacon for many years. France's Jeanne Calment, who died in 1997 at 122 and set the record for longevity, was a smoker.

There is one striking pattern among centenarians: They tend to have upbeat personalities.

None of which, Perls hastens to add, means we can all pig out and light up with impunity. Rather, it suggests that those of us destined to become centenarians possess special genes that make our tissues resistant to a wide array of insults.

There is one striking pattern among centenarians: They tend to have upbeat personalities. When I recently visited McCaig, the Massachusetts centenarian, she regaled me for over two hours with jolly stories, such as all the fun she'd had in the hospital making new friends after breaking her hip two years ago. When a reporter asked Calment at 115 how she saw her future, she replied with characteristic drollery: "Short, very short." Intriguingly, this lightness of being is a matter of temperament, which, because of other studies, scientists believe is determined largely by genes.

But even if great genes are key to extreme longevity, there might be too many of them to pin down as starting points to develop anti-aging drugs for the masses. Fortunately, Austad's weird old possums beg to differ.

Austad, a sinewy 52-year-old who worked as a Hollywood animal trainer before getting his Ph.D. in zoology, is the only gerontologist to have tangled with a lion while wearing a skirt and wig on an episode of the TV series *The Bionic Woman*. "The lion knocked me half goofy," says Austad, who was impersonating the show's heroine being attacked by the king of beasts. "Then it tried to mate with me.

Everyone on the set was roaring by the time they got it off me." Austad's foot also appeared in the same episode—it was shown getting stepped on by an elephant.

Austad became fascinated by the mystery of aging as a youth, when he watched his dog Spot pass from puppyhood to senility in 12 years. His curiosity was further piqued when he later learned how wildly variable life spans are. Tortoises can seem young at 150, and in a sense, they're immortal—they keep growing without physiological decline until disease, starvation, or people get them. Mice die around 2, yet bats, which resemble winged mice, can live into their 30s. Humans can live to at least 122, while the longevity record for the famously long-lived elephant is a mere 81.

It gradually dawned on Austad that the rate of aging is like tooth size—a highly plastic trait that evolution through the ages has readily dialed up or down to optimize fitness in different species. Rose's selective breeding of long-lived flies suggested an even more alluring idea: This plasticity exists within a species and can swiftly be brought into play by Darwinian forces favoring longevity. Rose, after all, didn't create mutant superflies—he simply coaxed into view a capacity for radical longevity that was hidden in normal flies' genes. Shortly after Rose's report, Austad set out to find similar life-span plasticity in higher animals.

He didn't have enough money and time to breed Methusaleh mammals in the lab—mimicking Rose's method with relatively long-lived animals might take decades. So he looked for a case in which nature had performed the experiment in the wild. He focused on opossums for two reasons: They age very fast, seldom living past two years, so cases of unusual longevity would be detectable fairly quickly. And he knew that since opossums were everywhere in the southeast U.S., he could probably find an isolated group on one of the region's many coastal islands.

It was a clever Darwinian ploy. Scientists believe the main reason animals such as turtles, bats, and humans are long-lived is that they possess strong defenses against predators—armor, flight, and smarts, respectively. That lets them reproduce over an extended period, which, in turn, has exerted evolutionary pressure to live longer—if we aged as fast as good old Spot, we'd miss out on a lot of the mating opportunities afforded by our imperviousness. In contrast, prey animals like mice and opossums have faced different evolutionary pressure: Since predators ensure they don't last long, it pays for them to make all the offspring they can ASAP and, in keeping with disposable-soma theory, let their cells wear out quickly.

But if such animals somehow landed on a predator-free island, Austad reasoned, evolution would push them toward greater longevity. After a long search, he found just the place: Sapelo Island, Ga. A small, largely deserted barrier island that geological records indicate separated from the mainland about 4,000 years ago, it's possum heaven. Austad found his subjects so oblivious to predators that they let him walk up to them in broad daylight and strap on radio collars. After monitoring the animals off and on for several years, he reported compelling evidence of life-span plasticity: the Sapelo Island opossums live, on average, about 25% longer than their mainland relatives. And they tend to have unusually small litters, as if they have traded fertility for longevity.

Austad's findings, detailed in his 1997 book *Why We Age,* generated little excitement in gerontology. His request for a grant to further study the island opossums was rejected. But to a few leading-edge thinkers, the report had a provocative implication: Aging may be a unitary process governed by a handful of key genes. One of those thinkers was Michigan's Miller, a pioneer in research on how the immune system ages.

> *Aging may be a unitary process governed by a handful of key genes.*

Miller is known for penning pithy rebuttals to the idea that genes don't matter much in aging. What especially impressed him about Austad's opossums was the speed at which their life expectancy had risen—their 4,000 years of island adaptation is an eye blink in evolutionary time.

Consider a dog analogy, he says. "The evolution of a big dog to a small one doesn't require mutation in the gene for leg size, the gene for kidney size, the gene for nose size, and so on." Otherwise, breeding, say, the first Chihuahua would have required a myriad of small-body mutations to have arisen simultaneously in one of the toy dog's larger forerunners—an event about as likely as typing chimps composing *Hamlet.* Instead, says Miller, small dogs evolved via a "twist of a genetic rheostat for size-of-things in the dog body." Similarly, evolution's invisible hand couldn't have swiftly slowed a myriad of unlinked age-related processes in the opossums. Instead, it probably twisted a rate-of-aging "pacemaker" regulated by a small set of genes.

The discovery in the late 1980s that worms' life spans can be doubled by a mutation in a single gene suggests that such pacemakers can be shockingly simple. Our pacemakers, if they exist, are likely to be more complex. Still, the extraordinary case of the Massachusetts family with five siblings near or over 100 suggests that inheriting no more than ten special genes may confer extreme longevity, says Perls, the Harvard centenarian researcher. It's simple probability: Because siblings get a different mix of genes from each parent, it's highly unlikely that the five siblings, and their seven centenarian cousins, would have drawn the same set of longevity-enabling genes if there were many more than ten involved.

But which genes twist the rheostat?

For answers, scientists are looking to one of gerontology's most tantalizing areas of research: life extension by caloric restriction, or CR. The phenomenon was first demonstrated in the 1930s, when one Clive McCay found that cutting rats' usual dietary calories by about a third extended their average life spans by up to 75%. It has been replicated in many species, most remarkably with Freddy, the longest-lived mouse on record. A resident of Harrison's lab in Maine, Freddy was nearly 5 when he died in 1987—lab mice normally live about two years.

As yet there's no proof that caloric restriction slows human aging, though a number of people are trying it. Many of them can be found on the Internet, endlessly chatting about food.

CR clearly isn't for the masses, but studies on it suggest what an anti-aging drug should do. "People used to think [CR] simply prevents cancer in lab animals," says Arlan Richardson, a CR expert at the University of Texas Health Science Center at San Antonio. "But now we think it actually affects the aging process. Probably 90% of the things that change with age are slowed down."

Indeed, CR's multitudinous benefits have proved almost as complex as the aging process itself, thwarting efforts to single out key metabolic changes that drive its life-extending effect. But the confusing welter began to fall into a coherent pattern after the calamitous shutdown of an air conditioner in Richardson's lab.

For a study on CR's effects, Richardson had set up a colony of mice in a hospital laboratory, including a group on restricted diets and a control group fed at will. One hot summer day, workers at a nearby construction project accidentally cut off electricity to the hospital wing housing the mice. When one of Richardson's colleagues arrived four hours later, many of the rodents had overheated and expired.

But something strange had happened: Some 80% of the well-fed control group were dead, compared with less than 25% of the CR mice. It was a classic case of serendipity. Richardson was interested in whether CR activates genes that make "heat-shock proteins," cellular guardian angels that help protect tissues from damage caused by heat and other kinds of stress. But he hadn't yet tested the idea. In effect, the construction workers had carried out an experiment that gave it strong support. In 1993, Richardson, with some trepidation about publicizing the accident, reported its results in a scientific journal.

The report helped trigger a flurry of studies on longevity and resistance to various insults, such as toxins, radiation, and heat. Over the next few years, a team led by Thomas Johnson, a University of Colorado researcher who studies life-extending mutations in nematodes, showed that long-living worms could survive a variety of stresses that kill normal ones.

Suddenly puzzle pieces were falling into place. Worm mutations that confer long life and stress resistance are known to help trigger a kind of suspended animation in nematodes called the dauer state. It begins when the nematodes sense, via chemical signals, that they're hemmed in by fellow worms—a cue that food is about to be in short supply. To Richardson and other researchers, the dauer state in worms looks a lot like what happens to mice on CR. In both cases, it appears that aging is slowed by revving up the "stress response," a complex system that includes genes for heat-shock proteins and antioxidant enzymes. The similarity also suggests why evolution seems to have favored life-span rheostats in many species: They've all had to cope with periodic food shortages, necessitating a mechanism that can retard aging when famine looms.

Johnson believes a vibrant stress response is crucial for healthy, long life in animals from worms to people. Indeed, centenarians may be born with stress-response genes permanently set on yellow alert—a possibility that's under intense scrutiny. San Antonio's Richardson is studying mice that have been genetically tweaked to boost certain stress-response genes activated by CR—if their lives are significantly extended, you can bet that stress genes will become hot, hot, hot.

The stress response, however, may well be just part of an array of "downstream" systems that rheostat master genes switch on to slow aging in higher animals. Three years ago, a little-known physiologist in Carbondale, Ill., named Andrzej Bartke blind-sided gerontologists with a breakthrough: The discovery of the first such mammalian master gene.

Bartke, a professor at Southern Illinois University, had been studying the effects of growth hormone. That's an urgent topic in the Corn Belt, for the hormone is given to cows to boost milk production. His team's experimental subjects were a race of giant mice implanted with extra growth-hormone genes. "When the animals are young, they look like supermouse, big and slick," he says. "But we noticed that they begin to get old and gray much sooner" than normal mice and live only about half as long. "So we thought, 'If more growth hormone means short life, maybe less of it means long life.'"

It was a radical idea. Bartke knew of a diminutive mutant mouse lacking growth hormone, called the Ames dwarf, but it was widely believed to show just the opposite tendency—supposedly it lived only a few months. Moreover, faddish physicians in places like Southern California routinely dispense growth hormone to older patients as an anti-aging elixir—it's claimed to help beef up muscles. But Bartke had worked with the dwarf mice, which are about the size of man's thumb, and knew the rumors of their early demise were greatly exaggerated. He also knew that within various species, including rats, horses, and humans, small body size is linked to longevity—tall men, for instance, appear more likely to get prostate cancer and other life-shortening diseases.

The pattern is most striking in dogs—giant breeds like Irish wolfhounds live only about six years, while toy breeds like Chihuahuas make it past ten. Fascinated by this pattern, Austad and other scientists theorized that when a life-span rheostat is set for slowed aging, it retards development early in life, when body size is being hormonally shaped.

Bartke's work added weight to the theory—and plausibility to the notion of life-span rheostats. In 1996 he reported that the dwarf mice live, on average, some 50% longer than their normal litter mates, and they seemed geared for famine—they won't reproduce without hormone shots, and they get so pudgy some researchers call them "butterball mice."

A rush of findings soon buttressed Bartke's discovery. Kevin Flurkey, a researcher with Harrison's group at Maine's Jackson Laboratory, showed that another strain of pudgy dwarf mice were similarly long lived. California Institute of Technology researchers identified a gene mutation in fruit flies, dubbed methusaleh, that revs their stress genes, fattens them up, and lengthens their average life spans by 35%. Ruvkun, the worm specialist in Boston, showed that a fattening, life-extending mutation in nematodes alters a gene that bears a striking resemblance to a human gene that's involved both in regulating blood sugar and growth.

The human gene, for the "insulin receptor," may be part of our rheostat circuitry. But fiddling with it is dangerous. When it's mutated in people, it appears to cause either morbid obesity or leprechaunism, a fatal syndrome in which growth is arrested at birth. Still, Ruvkun felt such cases could shed light on how the rheostat works: "I called around and asked endocrinologists whether they'd ever seen leprechauns that don't die soon after birth," he says. They hadn't.

That's not surprising. Mutating rheostat genes is like shorting out wires in an electric clock—it might run slower, but it's more likely to go haywire. Thus many researchers believe the best hope of pinpointing mammalian rheostat genes is to find a breed of metabolically normal, long-lived mice and study how they differ genetically from short-lived strains.

Soon after Bartke's report was published, Austad set out to do just that. Following the logic of his opossum study, he mounted an expedition to two remote Pacific islands, where he found a race of undersized mice. It's too early to say whether they possess anti-aging genes. But when crossed with purebred lab mice, they give birth to offspring that show a striking resemblance to long-lived British aristocrats—they reproduce later in life than most mice.

Meanwhile, Maine's Harrison crossed four strains of lab mice to produce the "Ancients," a breed that shows signs of slowed aging. Now he and Michigan's Miller are racing to pinpoint longevity-associated genes in such mice.

If the scientists succeed and the genes they find turn out to be analogues of ones that underlie longevity in worms, flies, and mice on CR, future historians will probably record the advance as the first time scientists lifted the cover off the life-span rheostat and peered at its wiring. And if the genes also resemble ones that researchers are racing to find in centenarians, gerontology may soon get its first Nobel prize.

It's hard to say how soon this grand scientific convergence could occur. Various researchers interviewed for this story hint that it's closer than anyone imagined only a year ago. "We are so much on the edge of major discoveries in this field," says Perls, who declines to elaborate on his latest centenarian findings until they're published in a scientific journal.

Translating the convergence into anti-aging medicines would doubtless take many years, and testing their efficacy wouldn't be easy. But perhaps it wouldn't take decades—it would be a matter of bioengineering, not magic, as with the bottled hogwash now sold to retard aging. Boston's Ruvkun adds that the rheostat quest appears to be leading to a handful of brain-produced hormones that govern the hibernation response. Though hormone therapy is notoriously tricky, he says, "if life span is hormonally regulated, it shouldn't be very hard to change it. I find that almost frightening. I think society would have a hard time coping with a rapid increase in life span."

True—to pay for all our extra years, we'd probably have to push early retirement out to age 80 or so. But who wants to spend 50 years playing golf, anyway?

The Sky's the Limit[2]

More and more members of America's over-50 set are into skydiving, rock climbing and other vigorous activities. What's age got to do with it? they ask. Not much, the experts say.

BY BETTI JANE LEVINE
LOS ANGELES TIMES, FEBRUARY 5, 1998

Mildred Hunter has always wanted to soar. But what with one thing and another (two marriages, raising a child and full-time work) she never got the chance.

So five years ago, at 75, Hunter took the plunge. She began skydiving in tandem with her son, Bob.

"It's so exciting each time that I can hardly wait to go back," Hunter reports from a Houston hospital bed—where she's nursing a broken leg acquired in her most recent parachute jump. Within the last year, the 80-year-old Hunter has also gone up in a hot air balloon, taken a glider ride and ventured aloft in a paraplane.

"I'm going to live it up as much as I can for as long as I can," she says. "My age has nothing to do with it."

Hunter is representative of thousands of the venturesome mature, part of what may be called the "new old" population of America. These are the millions of people who have passed well beyond the half-century mark and don't think twice about it. Blessed with good health, they continue to do what they've always done, or what they've always wanted to do.

They are surprising even the experts who have been predicting all this.

Dr. Terrie Wetle was skiing down an Oregon mountainside recently and stopped at a lodge for food.

"I saw this bunch of old people finishing lunch. They looked to be in their 70s and 80s," Wetle says. "I watched them leave, put on their skis, and go down that big mountain so beautifully that I was amazed. It was a kind of confirmation."

Wetle, 51, is a grandmother, gerontologist and deputy director of the National Institute on Aging. She intends to ski "for another 20 or 30 years" and believes she'll be part of a crowd of her peers.

Because despite the snipes and jeers of the under-50 set, those who have passed that mythical landmark are shining in all sorts of activities and sports, extreme and otherwise.

Is America ready for that? No way. After Sonny Bono died on the slopes at 62, and Sen. John Glenn (D-Ohio) announced that he'll travel into space again at 77, radio talk shows were awash with jokes and comments from listeners repulsed that "geezers" are risking their lives in such dangerous ways. One caller couldn't understand why old people, "who've already had their day," would do anything risky at all. "What are they trying to prove?"

He can be forgiven for not understanding. On one hand, America is aware that people are living longer, healthier lives with every passing decade (life expectancy has climbed to 76.1 years). They know that with gene therapy and other breakthroughs, the longevity statistics will almost surely continue to improve.

... despite the snipes and jeers of the under-50 set, those who have passed that mythical landmark are shining in all sorts of activities and sports, extreme and otherwise.

On the other hand, many Americans still believe anyone older than 50 is old. Anyone older than 60 is very old. And anyone older than 70 is fragile, diminished mentally and physically, and should be on wheels, a cane or in a pine box. They believe it because the popular culture has told them to.

Most Americans have not yet heard about "successful aging," a concept born 10 years ago as the result of a research program supported by the MacArthur Foundation. Dr. John D. Rowe, the principal investigator, concluded that medical research has placed too much emphasis on the deficits that come with aging and were always thought to be caused by the aging process itself.

Rowe showed, through various studies, that these declines may really be explained in terms of lifestyle, habits, diet and an array of psychosocial factors having nothing to do with the aging process.

In other words, while getting old does cause physiological changes of all sorts, it does not cause the mental and physical declines that have always been associated with age, he says. If no disease is present, a healthy old person can be expected to continue the same activities as when he or she was younger, although not necessarily on the same level.

"A revolutionary increase in life span has already occurred," Rowe wrote in a 1987 *Science* magazine article. "A corresponding increase in health span and the maintenance of full function as nearly as possible to the end of life" is the goal doctors and older Americans must now set for themselves.

Bill Jones is already on this course. At 66, he climbs mountains, skis, skydives and is an active rancher in Utah. He flies planes for business and pleasure, and just bought an airport in Alaska, where he plans to start a tourist business.

"I don't perceive myself as young or old. I am what I am—an active, interested person. I see no reason not to continue to be that," he says. "Of course, I can't bench press 300 pounds anymore, but I can certainly continue to function in the world I've created for myself. You don't die when you hit 60. People ask me all the time, 'Are you still doing all that?' I say of course. And I plan to continue."

So does Patrick Moorehead, 66, of Long Beach. He is president of Skydivers Over 60, a group formed in 1992 "as a kind of lark." It now has more than 400 members, he says. Moorehead retired at 50 from his job as a fire department battalion chief "because the job was inherently dangerous." But he maintains his lifestyle, including a healthy diet and regular exercise—both mental and physical—and he jumps at least 10 times a month and participates in skydiving competitions all over the world.

"I don't perceive myself as young or old. I am what I am—an active, interested person. I see no reason not to continue to be that." —66-year-old retiree Bill Jones

Moorehead says he's "frankly disappointed in the amount of people that succumb to advancing years. My wife and I just got back from Las Vegas. We saw so many people who have let themselves deteriorate, who seem to have no interest in physical activity that will keep them healthy and in shape. They are doing themselves a disservice," he says, because "they perceive themselves as society perceives them. They think once you get past that certain milestone that society calls old age, you must back down from life. What a waste."

Dr. Robert Butler, founding director of the National Institute on Aging and now chief executive of the International Longevity Center and professor at Mount Sinai School of Medicine in New York, agrees.

"I remember George Bush's skydive, at 72, got so much attention that I was asked to discuss it on TV shows," Butler says. "But the truth is many people much older than Bush are doing the same or similar things. It's not talked about because it's still not socially acceptable" to be so active at an advanced age, Butler says.

"Although our population is growing older, the rates of disability are declining. In other words, people are vigorous and healthy longer than they used to be. Someone 80 today may be the equivalent of a 60-year-old in the last century. Part of the decline is physiological. But the big constraint is sociological," he says. That's because the reaction of people is still relatively negative, Butler says.

"My point is, the sociology may not yet have caught up with the physiology. An older person has to be very careful about being looked upon as too sexy, or too vigorous, or too interested in life because society may frown upon such people."

The experts seem to agree that America is in a state of transition. The "old old" group still sees themselves as they used to see their own grandparents: frail and decaying. Many who have had a lifetime of poor nutrition and little physical activity accept as inevitable the physical consequences of their choices and incorrectly consider the results to be a normal part of aging.

The "new old" population consists of people who have led active and healthy lifestyles, who have benefited from recent medical

---

The "new old" population consists of people who have led active and healthy lifestyles, who have benefited from recent medical advances or are simply genetically blessed with good health in advanced age.

---

advances or are simply genetically blessed with good health in advanced age. They are the cutting edge of what experts say will soon be considered the norm.

The theory of "successful aging" is not just a theory, Butler says. It's happening quietly every day. "Consider this: On any given day in America, of all our population over 65, 81% are doing more than OK physically." By that he means, they are independent and fully functional.

And gerontologist Wetle reports that "the old assumption that loss of mental abilities is a natural part of aging has now been proven false. We now know that some people lose memory and the ability to reason, but those losses are always caused by disease." The primary and growing example of this is Alzheimer's disease. Those with no disease do not lose their faculties in old age, she says, although society believes otherwise. And as medical science is able to eradicate more age-associated disease, an even bigger segment of the population will retain full faculties into very old age, she predicts.

Robert Ward Parker, 75, maintains status quo on all fronts. The Santa Fe, N.M., resident lives minutes from the mountains, where he skis "a minimum of twice a week," often with a group of men who are his age or older. His friend Robert Nordhaus, 88, skied with him until this year, when a "minor physical setback" took him off the slopes.

A member of the 10th Mountain Division of the U.S. Army during World War II, Parker was in the elite force that fought on skis in mountain terrain. The members of the 10th have remained buddies and athletes ever since, with many of them instrumental in founding outdoor survival groups and such ski resorts as Vail, Colo., Parker says.

In 1995, he organized his buddies for a trip to Europe, where they repeated climbing a 2,000-foot mountain in the Appenines; they climbed it the first time in 1945.

"Seven veterans, ages 72 to 80, climbed to the top again," Parker says. This time they were joined in friendship by some of the German and Italian mountain troops they had once fought. "It was a wonderful experience," he says.

He also rock climbs, writes poetry and engages in what he calls "independent archeological research that involves miles and miles of walking in rough country, usually by myself. I've made three discoveries that no one else has made in this state where so many archeologists are working," he says with pride. These days, he's working on an "astrological alignment of stone structures in eastern New Mexico." If he confirms the alignments, he'll submit the data to an archaeo-astronomical journal, he says.

My body functions as if I were a normal 55-year old. And mentally, I'm still a teenager in terms of wanting to explore the world."
—75-year-old Robert Ward Parker

His view of aging? "I think of myself as maybe 35. My body functions as if I were a normal 55-year old. And mentally, I'm still a teenager in terms of wanting to explore the world."

Parker and so many others like him are what Butler predicts will be typical of old people in America's very near future.

"When the baby boomers reach Golden Pond, they are going to transform the image of old age. It will be a much more vigorous, active and vibrant period of life," Butler says. "The boomers will be physically active and continue to work longer. We can't have 40 million people sitting around doing nothing. It's a waste. That's really the main point of all this.

"It's not just skiing and jumping out of planes—but continuing to contribute to our society. Have you heard about the airline pilots? They're fighting to fly past the age of 60."

Baby Boom's New Wrinkle[3]

A Rush to Cosmetic Surgery

By Sharon Walsh
Washington Post, March 12, 1998

Business is booming for Denise Thomas, a cosmetic surgery consultant who takes clients doctor-shopping for just the right surgeon to laser away wrinkles, get rid of droopy eyelids, suction out fat or tighten up that turkey gobbler neck.

Her appointment book contains the names of Wall Street vice presidents, physicians, lawyers, graphic artists and museum curators who believe they need, as well as want, a youthful, vigorous appearance. Many of them are from the army of 76 million baby boomers marching reluctantly through middle age and are willing to endure expensive and painful procedures to look younger. Plastic surgery, at one time the province of the rich and famous, has become the refuge of the merely middle class and the barely old. While widespread acceptance of the nip and tuck has been growing over the last decade, its use has mushroomed in a climate of rising disposable income and the baby boomers' fear of aging. Once the goal was to look more beautiful. Now, experts say, it is to stay young-looking.

"A lot of the baby boomers have the money and they are fighting like hell to stay young, especially the men," Thomas said. "It's been a very big year. A wonderful year. And I think next year will be even better."

Statistics show that the number of men and women in the United States having cosmetic surgery has increased by 75 percent in the past four years and that both sexes are undergoing procedures at younger ages than in the past. In New York state, more than 91,000 cosmetic procedures were performed in 1996, according to the American Society of Plastic and Reconstructive Surgeons.

At the Manhattan Eye, Ear and Throat Hospital, the largest cosmetic surgery hospital in the world, the number of cosmetic surgeries so far this year is up 20 percent over last year. "We have seven or

---

eight operating rooms going every day, and it's sometimes hard to schedule procedures," said Sherrell Aston, chairman of the department of plastic surgery at the hospital.

According to the plastic surgeons' group, many people are having eye lifts, tummy tucks or liposuction in their thirties or forties rather than waiting for their fifties. Take tummy tucks. In 1992, 58 percent of those having tummy tucks were between 35 and 50. Four years later, that age group had only 32 percent of the tummy tucks performed while those in the 19 to 34 age group getting them leaped from 19 percent to 33 percent.

The number of men having liposuction—the country's No. 1 plastic surgery procedure—and eye lifts has gone up steadily across the country. And, the experts said, the number of women climbing the corporate ladder who come in for surgery also has boomed.

"I've done 5,000 anti-aging procedures in the last 20 years," said Gerald Imber, a plastic surgeon who said the majority of his patients are professional people. "I think that now maintenance is really the name of the game." Women "can look virtually unchanged" between the ages of 35 and 50, he said.

"I'm not of the mind that you should grow old gracefully." — facelift recipient **Theodora Pappas**

Theodora Pappas, a fiftyish graphic designer, had a face lift on Jan. 28. "Most of the people I work with in the publishing industry are barely out of diapers," Pappas said. "A few are in their thirties. I'm young in outlook... . But when I looked in the mirror and found droopy lids and stuff hanging under my chin, I looked like my mother. There was too much of a disparity between how I felt and how I looked... I'm not of the mind that you should grow old gracefully. Forget it."

Aleta St. James, a New York counselor specializing in emotional healing, had an eye lift when she was 40. Now 50, she recently had a mini-face lift.

"I'm in the public and do a lot of speaking," said St. James, a former actress who once had the lead in the musical *Hair*. "My whole concept is that your body should reflect your spirit. I take care of myself, but certain things just happen. You still age."

Young and fresh, in other words, is becoming more important than being beautiful.

"No one wants to look like they're too old and tired to do the job," said Donald B. Giddon, clinical professor of behavioral science at New York University. "It's probably job specific. But the public's perception of age is that with age comes memory loss," Giddon said. "People assume that if you look older, you have lost some brain power."

"I had a woman come in recently who's just 40, but she works at one of the big museums and was frightened of losing her job," said cosmetic surgery consultant Thomas. "She's having a face lift, and she considers it an investment in her business."

Men come in with specific requests—to get rid of bags under their eyes or sagging jowls—but they still want to keep their liposuction of love handles or eye lifts quiet, preferring that people think they've just been on a long vacation, said George Beraka, who teaches surgery at Cornell Medical College. "Men fear they'll be considered effeminate if they care too much about how they look," he said.

Charles Cardany, a plastic surgeon in Chevy Chase who did St. James's surgery, said that New Yorkers are not alone in their rush to the surgeon's office. Washington has its fair share of cosmetic surgery patients, many of whom tell Cardany they are coming in before changing jobs. "They usually want to keep it very quiet," he said. "We check them in under pseudonyms sometimes or often cosmetic outpatient units have private entrances."

> *"Men fear they'll be considered effeminate if they care too much about how they look."*
> —Dr. George Beraka, Cornell Medical College

Costs vary widely depending on where the patient has the surgery done and the expertise of the surgeon, but whether it's a $4,000 eye lift or a $20,000 face lift, the money doesn't seem to be a stumbling block.

"I have a patient right now in her forties who is having a face lift and transferring money from a mutual fund," said Cardany. "She saved the money for this."

Cosmetic surgery is more common now in part because it has become safer. New techniques, such as laser resurfacing to remove wrinkles or sun damage, and endoscopic surgery, which leaves only a pin-prick of a scar, have revolutionized some procedures, surgeons said.

"Cosmetic surgery just works," said Aston. "And when a certain number of people have had it and their friends see how good they look, the word spreads." The search for the perfect face is not without controversy, however. Two stories that have enthralled New Yorkers recently involve cosmetic surgery. In one, Columbia-Presbyterian Medical Center was forced to close its plastic surgery division after state health officials learned that its residents were secretly performing cosmetic surgery without supervision for cash.

In another case, Jocelyn Wildenstein, the soon-to-be-ex-wife of one of the world's wealthiest art collectors, became the butt of New York jokes because of her many plastic surgeries. *The New York Daily News* called her "The Bride of Wildenstein" because of the procedures that turned the face of a beautiful woman into a catlike sphere and left her looking as if she couldn't blink. A New York judge last week awarded her $2 million a year in alimony but decreed she couldn't use any of it for cosmetic surgery.

Moreover, those who are going for the youthful look find that it does not come easily or cheaply.

Pappas's face lift was no party. During 7 1/2 hours of surgery, the doctor took care of her upper eyes, the bags under her lower lids, the lines from her nose to her mouth, droopy skin under her chin and little pouches around her mouth.

"As things went south, I got fat pads in my jaw. They moved it up to my cheeks," Pappas said. "Now my cheekbones feel like the tail fins on a 1955 Cadillac, but they look great and there are no scars!"

The new look cost her $15,000 for the surgeon, $1,800 for private duty nurses, $1,400 for the hospital, $1,050 for the anesthesia and $379 a night for a hotel suite where she and a private nurse stayed for several days. (In most cosmetic surgery the patient is released from the hospital hours after the procedure but needs around-the-clock care for days while on pain medication.) Her grand total: more than $20,000.

For days after the surgery, her face felt several times its normal size. Her eyes were swollen nearly shut. She had two drains coming out of her head and was groggy from the pain killers and anesthetic.

"It was like having a pumpkin face with Garfield eyes," said Pappas of the way she felt when she looked in the mirror after her surgery. For those who have full face lifts, the swelling may not go away completely for many months.

"If I had known what it was going to be like for the first four days, I probably wouldn't have had it done," Pappas said. "I don't know yet what the long-term impact of it will be. But I know that I feel better about myself."

Let's Hear It For Decrepitude[4]

BY MELVIN MADDOCKS
NEW YORK TIMES, AUGUST 27, 1999

Like most 70-somethings, I can't pick up a magazine or tune into a talk show without encountering somebody much younger telling me what a great time of life I've arrived at.

In fact, all the wild enthusiasm about the joys of being "mature" is really aimed at baby boomers, who live in terror of ending up, heaven forbid, like their parents.

Do they honestly believe that you're only as old as you think you are? Are they really convinced they can remain "forever young" (as a *Time* cover story put it) if they think positively, jog faithfully and eat tons of broccoli?

Of course not. Baby boomers may be charter members of the Me Forever generation, but they're also secret hypochondriacs, panicked about their genes, ominously well-informed about the rarest diseases. The best may be yet to come, but in the meantime, please pass the Prozac.

Why should these outsiders define old age for us, the natives—and worse, prescribe their recipe for our happiness? Just consider the banal advice they bombard us with, like "Keep active," an exhortation almost as meaningless as "Have a nice day." Who would argue for being inactive?

Behind the strategy of keeping old coots busy and off the streets—for their own good, of course—we detect a sneaky attempt to phase old age out of existence by making it an extension of middle age, pretending the so-called new friskiness is the norm. Every man ready to take his parachute and jump like George Bush. Every woman preparing, like the poet Judith Viorst, to celebrate her 70th birthday by acquiring a tattoo.

Doesn't it occur to those prodding us toward the finish line that there's a subtle cruelty in asking us to "stay in the fast lane" and "go for it" at 70-something as we did at 30-something?

Old age, it seems, is two different countries. There's real old age, for those of us who live there, and, on the whole, like it. At least so far. Then there's old age for middle-aged control freaks—a fantasy

---

land where organ transplants and a biochemical fountain of youth bubbling with superhormones will cure old age before baby boomers reach it.

Yes, people today enjoy better health and live longer. But does that mean a revolution is taking place? Life expectancy has been increasing since Cicero declared that old age began at 46, and a 46-year-old living to be 76 is more of a miracle than a 76-year-old living to be 106. Compared with eternal life—the promise of most religions—the virtual immortality promised by our new secular alternative only qualifies as a stingy second helping.

On the brink of old age, Freud confessed, "Strange, secret yearnings rise in me for a life of quite another kind." Did even Freud know exactly what he meant? But he voiced the cry from the heart of a 70-something: Let me grow old—let me grow up. Give me one last chance to take life seriously.

I don't expect to convince baby boomers of my conviction that if they bowdlerize the final chapter they'll miss out on the fullness of life in all its mystery, its sweetness, its terror. On the other hand, the boomers shouldn't count on converting us to their credo on modern immaturity, based as it is on the simplistic assumption that being young is the same as being happy.

Just Desserts[5]

BY HILA COLMAN
NEW YORK TIMES MAGAZINE, MAY 3, 1998

As a child I was content to have my time planned for me. School, piano lessons on Tuesday, dancing classes on Thursday, and Saturday mornings (a loony idea of my mother's) something called elocution lessons. I remember a lot of deep breathing and loud and embarrassing yodeling.

When I got to high school, however, a new need appeared. I wanted something I called time for myself. I hadn't counted on all that homework, the push for extracurricular activities (they will look good on my application for college, my teachers said) and a sudden interest in boys, clothes and fiddling with my hair. By the time I got to college, I knew leisure was out. But I still dreamed of an occasional lazy afternoon and being stretched out on a hammock. Maybe when I got married, I thought. Where did I ever get such an outlandish notion? I had to clean the house, launder the clothes, shop for groceries, cook meals and take care of two young boys, in addition to working long hours at home on my writing. The eternal optimist, I did buy the hammock, but it and my back never met.

I am not complaining. I look back on a life that was rich— full of love and rewards, even in hard times. But peaceful and leisurely, not exactly.

On my 80th birthday, my family and friends gave me a lovely party. They congratulated me and said with straight faces that I looked 60. I thanked them, but thought to myself, I was no beauty at 60, why should I want to look like that now?

Moreover, why should I want to be young now? As my grandchildren say, "Been there, done that." Yet, I am being hit from all sides with things I must do, foods I must eat, ways I must think to stay forever young. I get exhausted just thinking about it. First I have to have a project—quilting, rug-hooking or painting pretty watercolors. Better yet, I should go to classes where I'll meet people and exercise my brain; perhaps study Eastern religions or the history of tapestry. For God's sake, didn't I have enough of sitting in classrooms?

Think positive, be upbeat, they say, and this bunch of vitamins will help. (Even though, after spending your money, you may be told that the rules have changed and you took the wrong ones.)

Working out in a gym is a must. I tried it once and was told by a gorgeous 30-year-old woman that my posture was lousy (I knew that) and that a woman my age should be careful on the machines. I was careful enough not to go back.

There are other ways to search for youth after the age of 70. You can spend lots of money and many hours in a beauty salon changing the color of your hair, and even get lured into wearing short skirts and hobble on high heels to look youthful. You can hand your retirement money over to a plastic surgeon for a few tucks around the eyes or the chin or both. Or buy some magic cream that will supposedly erase those wrinkles. Not me. I am rather fond of my wrinkles. They get me a seat on the bus and a discount at the movies.

I want my old age to be different from my youth, not just a continuation of it. Old age is a new experience. I've never been there before. I have never had the luxury of not having to do anything. No commitment, no demand on my time.

I want my old age to be different from my youth, not just a continuation of it.

I rather fancy my days, languid stretches of time out of a gothic Southern novel. In the morning I can snuggle back under my luscious down comforter and get up when I please. After breakfast, I go to the post office to get my mail. Living alone in the country, I find this to be the high point of my day. If anyone offers to get my mail, I say no. I want the fun of stopping to visit friends, to gossip, to argue our local politics. I am in no hurry. I don't have to run off to a job or a meeting.

I might answer some letters, pay bills, glance at catalogues or write—at the typewriter. No computer here. A sandwich, a cup of tea, a siesta, then a long walk along a nearby lake might round out my day until dinner.

Uneventful? Yes. But taken in the context of a life that always had a time schedule, always had an unending list of things to do, my day is a gift from the gods. Each age has been different, and I have enjoyed them all. I am not going to waste this age by trying to skip it.

My life now is my dessert, the whipped cream of leisure I was longing for. It probably sounds empty to many, and not useful, but I am tired of being useful. This is my time to enjoy the quietness of just being, of stopping to look and feel and think, of indulging myself. Time for myself at last.

III. Elder Care—A Few Options

Editor's Introduction

Changes in family life and increasing life spans have created a dilemma for many Americans: how to provide care for elderly parents or relatives when they become unable to care for themselves. According to statistics published in *Time,* in 1999 about 30 percent of Americans 65 and older lived alone; 54 percent lived with their spouse; roughly 13 percent lived with relatives; and a little more than 2 percent lived with nonrelatives. Thus, the majority of older Americans live independently or as couples. Of those living alone, some receive help from programs—services that deliver meals to their homes, for instance—designed to enable elderly people to live on their own longer.

As Americans reach their 80s, however, it becomes far more likely that they will come to depend on others to help care for them. As of the late 1990s, for example, one in four American families were caring for an elderly relative, and an estimated 43 percent of seniors could expect to spend some time in a nursing home during their lifetimes. This chapter provides a look at three major care options: receiving care from relatives, nursing homes, and assisted living facilities. Although finding quality care for the elderly is not a new problem, few families find perfect solutions, and new alternatives are still being sought. Some of the most recent and innovative of these, including adult day care and foster care programs, could not be covered in this book. For an article that discusses the latter type of program, please see "Home and Not Alone: a Foster Care Program for Grown-Ups" (*New York Times*) in the abstracts section.

Many families prefer not to entrust strangers with the care of an older relative. Especially in the cases of aging parents or grandparents, many of whom provided care for their now-adult children when both groups were younger, people feel it is their duty to care for relatives themselves. Having an older relative live at home however, particularly in cases in which the person needs help with basic daily activities, can become exhausting for the caretaker. This is markedly true of the so-called "sandwich-generation"—those who are "sandwiched" between the responsibilities of caring for both their own children and an elderly parent or relative. As Sara Rimer reports in "Blacks Carry Load of Care for Their Elderly" (*New York Times*), African-American families are especially likely to take on the care of older family members. For all families, Rimer writes, "While caring for one's own is a source of pride, and a statement of love and obligation, it also carries costs in terms of stress, lost wages, jobs and educational opportunities passed up, as well as health risks to the care-givers."

Assisted living is among the newer choices available to those seeking care for an older adult. Just as the name would imply, such facilities offer elderly residents more care and supervision than they would have living on their own or, in most cases, with their relatives, but without the more intensive medical care and higher costs associated with nursing homes. They may also provide privacy and a sense of both independence and community that seniors living with relatives may lack. In "Elder Care: Making the Right Choice" (*Time*), John Greenwald provides a good introduction to the topic of assisted living by giving an overview of the ranges of service, styles of facilities, and typical costs involved.

Nursing homes, though often the best equipped to care for elderly people who are ill or need around-the-clock care or supervision, are expensive and have gained a reputation for being impersonal and, in some scandal-provoking cases, even negligent. As we see in another article by Sara Rimer, "Seattle's Elderly Find a Home for Living, Not Dying" (*New York Times*), Providence-Mount St. Vincent is "widely regarded to be what many Americans consider an impossibility: a good nursing home." Due largely to the management's ethos and the exceptional staff at the Mount, as the home is called, inhabitants there are better off than those at many other facilities around the country. But as successful as the Mount is, Rimer writes, "it cannot alter the stark realities of aging that its residents confront every day: the spouses, friends, and even children outlived, the physical limitations, the loss of independence and control."

No matter the options available for elder care, now and in the future, the decisions families face as members age may always be fraught with anxiety. The choice as to where aging relatives should spend their last years can be a difficult compromise at best—between the family members involved, as well as between alternatives, each of which has both benefits and drawbacks. In the case of Cynthia Kaplan's family, the choice was a clear one. Her grand-mother, suffering from Alzheimer's disease, had to be put in a nursing home. Still, in her op-ed essay entitled "Better, Safer, Warmer" (*New York Times*), Kaplan recalls the anguish she felt in doing what she knew to be in her grand-mother's best interests. "It feels like the most violent act in which I have ever participated," she writes. "I would take it back, if I could."

Blacks Carry Load of Care for Their Elderly[1]

By Sara Rimer
NEW YORK TIMES, March 15, 1998

Eldora Mitchell is nearly as old as the century, and for her it has been a life of love and service, starting at the age of 12, when she went to work scrubbing white people's floors to help her family. Later, she cleaned hospital rooms to feed her own children and cared for her grandchildren while their parents were working. In her 60s, she nursed her dying husband and her elderly mother.

Now, at 95, frail and slowly going blind, it is Mrs. Mitchell's turn. Four years ago, she moved across town to her retirement home—a bedroom in her son Charles's house here, with bright green curtains and her large-print Bible on the nightstand.

Mrs. Mitchell collects $568 a month in Social Security and a pension of $45 a month from Duke Medical Center, where she retired from the housekeeping department. She has about $8,000 in savings and no long-term health insurance. What she does have is her family, and her expectation—redeemed by their promises—that they will do for her as she has done for previous generations.

The Mitchells are following a tradition in the African-American community, where families have long been expected to care for their mothers and fathers and grandparents, as well as for their children. It is a tradition born of "certain harsh realities," as Jacqueline Jones, a historian, puts it, "of a historic lack of access to good medical care, public support and the kind of jobs that guaranteed a secure old age."

Peggye Dilworth-Anderson, a sociologist and gerontologist at the University of North Carolina at Greensboro, is directing a four-year study of African-Americans in the state who are caring for relatives. "There are lots of Mr. Mitchells," Dr. Dilworth-Anderson said.

The tradition is hardly unique to blacks. Studies show that nearly one in four American families is taking care of an elderly relative or friend, doing everything from changing diapers to shopping for groceries. With the ranks of those who are known as "the old old" growing ever larger, and the Federal Government consid-

---

ered unlikely to provide help in the form of a comprehensive long-term care program any time soon, more and more families are expected to find themselves taking care of elderly relatives.

Still, older blacks are twice as likely as whites to receive care from family members when their health declines, according to a recent study for the National Institute on Aging by Dr. Raymond T. Coward, dean of health and human services at the University of New Hampshire.

And while caring for one's own is a source of pride, and a statement of love and obligation, it also carries costs in terms of stress, lost wages, jobs and educational opportunities passed up, as well as health risks to the caregivers.

"It's a labor of love, but it exacts a tremendous toll from people who have few resources to begin with," said Dr. Jones, a professor of Afro-American and labor history at Brandeis University and the

---

. . . older blacks are twice as likely as whites to receive care from family members when their health declines, according to a recent study for the National Institute on Aging by Dr. Raymond T. Coward, dean of health and human services at the University of New Hampshire.

---

author of *American Work: Four Centuries of Black and White Labor.*

In fact, given the economic stresses on black families, and their increased mobility, some experts worry that coming generations will be unable to take on the caregiving role.

"There is a gap between the cultural value and what is practical," said Rose C. Gibson, a gerontologist and professor emeritus at the University of Michigan, who has studied the black elderly.

The statistics highlight the need: Older blacks have more than double the rate of poverty of older whites, and they suffer from far more health problems, according to figures from the Census Bureau. They have higher rates of hypertension, asthma and diabetes and require more help with the tasks of daily living.

Yet there is more of a resistance to institutional care among blacks than whites, experts say. Years ago, discrimination and poverty barred blacks from nursing homes, or rest homes, as assisted-living facilities are known in North Carolina. The ones they could afford, when they did gain entry, often offered minimal care at best. Among African-Americans, stories abound of relatives and friends mistreated in nursing homes. While the options have improved —at least for the middle class—there remains a deep, cultural mistrust of institutions for the elderly.

Gloria Roberson, a retired University of North Carolina accounting clerk, spent nearly every waking moment for five years caring for her mother, who had Alzheimer's disease, at home in Chapel Hill. Her doctor, concerned about the burden she was taking on, urged her to consider a nursing home, Mrs. Roberson recalled. "We just don't do that," she said. "Not with our people."

Financially, some elderly blacks have no option other than entering a nursing home under the Medicaid program, the Federal health care program for the poor. Blacks are far less likely than whites to have spouses to help with their care.

Thirty-four percent of blacks older than 65 live in multigenerational homes, compared with 18 percent of whites.

It is not an easy burden for the younger generation. Black caregivers tend to have less money than most white families caring for an elderly relative, so they bear a disproportionately higher burden of the care themselves because they can not afford to hire help.

They are also much more likely to have the additional responsibility of children at home. More than half of all black caregivers have one or more children younger than 18 at home, compared with 39 percent of white caregivers. Many of the black caregivers are single working mothers. Thirty-four percent of blacks older than 65 live in multigenerational homes, compared with 18 percent of whites.

Rewarding Payback From a Caring Son

Charles Mitchell was in the kitchen, cooking supper for his mother. It was 3 p.m., eight hours before he would clock in at his paid job. A police dispatcher at North Carolina Central University in Durham, he works the graveyard shift so he can spend his days looking after his mother. Most black caregivers, studies show, hold regular jobs.

"Some of my friends say, 'You're something else, man,'" said Mr. Mitchell, who is 55 and divorced. "They say they admire what I'm doing. I say, 'Well, this is mom. I don't have but one.' She brought me up and looked after me. I feel I should do the same. I feel everybody should."

Mrs. Mitchell said of her son: "I can do for myself. He don't have to wait on me."

But wait on her he does. Three times a day he puts medicated drops in his mother's eyes. He empties the commode in her bedroom that she uses at night. He changes the sheets on her bed. He washes her back, as she did for him when he was small, as she did for her mother when she was old and blind.

He barely mentions his own health problems. A diabetic, Mr. Mitchell injects himself with insulin daily.

For all the talk about the so-called disintegrating black family, what is often ignored is the strength of the extended family. "That's the irony," Dr. Jones said. "People are constantly denigrating black family life. But if you look at how these families survive and sustain themselves over the generations it's a testament to their strength and resilience."

> *For all the talk about the so-called disinte-grating black family, what is often ignored is the strength of the extended family.*

Mr. Mitchell has no paid home health care aides or housekeepers to help with his mother. But he has the support of family members and friends.

His sister Audrey, 52, who also lives in Durham, spends nights with their mother while Mr. Mitchell is working. His other sister, Mildred, 54, who lives nearby, comes by regularly to fix her mother's hair and provide other intimate care. Mr. Mitchell's girlfriend, Sheila Parker, helps with cooking and housework.

The Mitchells' caregiving arrangement is typical of African-American families, Dr. Dilworth-Anderson has found in her study, which is being financed by the National Institute on Aging.

That legacy is particularly strong in the tradition-minded South. Dr. Dilworth-Anderson says she has found that whether caregivers live in urban Durham or rural Warren County, whether their income is $15,000 or $50,000 a year, the sense of obligation is similar.

"What varies is how they can express that sense of obligation," said Dr. Dilworth-Anderson, a professor in the department of human development and family studies. "A high-powered lawyer may have enough resources to make sure her mother is cared for well by using formal services. In that way she feels she's living up to her sense of duty. The lower-class woman may say, 'I don't have all this money to hire all these people, but I have my sisters and brothers.'"

The caregivers are strongly motivated by faith, Dr. Dilworth-Anderson said. "You get cultural reinforcement from your neighbors, your friends, from the church," she said.

Two Mothers First, Husband Second

For Martha Perry, caregiving meant pulling up stakes in New Jersey, giving up her job and her daily life with her husband, deferring her own dreams.

Four years ago, Mrs. Perry, 49, who had been a supervisor at a group home for the disabled, returned to the town of Wendell, near Raleigh, and moved in with her elderly mother-in-law, who had advanced diabetes. Mrs. Perry's husband, a postal worker, is the family's main breadwinner, and they could not afford for him to leave his job.

There were also other considerations that prompted Mrs. Perry, who has a 24-year-old son, to join the ranks of caregivers, the majority of whom are women. Mrs. Perry said her husband told her, "I can't bathe her, I can't do the things for her that you can do."

Mrs. Perry took her mother-in-law, Maggie Perry, to the hospital for dialysis three times a week, lifting her and her wheelchair in and out of her car. She gave her mother-in-law insulin injections, cooked for her and bathed her.

Mrs. Perry said her husband and his four brothers paid her $200 a week. A home health aide spent two hours at the house two or three days a week. Eventually, Maggie Perry had to have a leg amputated and was placed in a nursing home, where she died in January of kidney failure.

The demands on Martha Perry have been unrelenting. She had to stay in North Carolina to care for her mother, Eula Brodie, who is 85 and unable to live on her own. For six months, Mrs. Perry was a round-the-clock caregiver, living with her mother near Raleigh.

She was eventually able to move her mother into the nearby McKissick Center, an assisted-living center. The move allowed Mrs. Perry to go back to work, as a group home manager for disabled adults.

Mrs. Brodie, the daughter of sharecroppers, had worked as a maid and a home health care aide until she was 80. She receives about $1,000 a month from Social Security and her pension, Mrs. Perry said.

The McKissick Center had been charging her $1,600 a month. For about a year, Mrs. Perry paid half the cost herself and half out of her mother's monthly income. Two weeks ago, the center learned that Mrs. Perry, unable to afford the cost, was about to quit her job and move her mother back home and reduced her mother's monthly fee to $1,150.

Mrs. Perry has five brothers and seven sisters, who live scattered across the country. They shared a chaotic, harsh childhood, Mrs. Perry said, and have not forgiven their mother for it. Together, they send about $500 a month to help with her expenses, Mrs. Perry said.

"I love my mother because I saw her working herself to death so we could eat," said Mrs. Perry, who visits her mother regularly and oversees her care.

But now it is Mrs. Perry who is exhausted. "I'll be honest," she said. "Sometimes it's tempting to just walk away. This is taking its toll on my health. I have hypertension. I'm just tired of it, I'm so tired. I've had days where I've said, 'Please, Lord, take her.'"

Her husband, who is 65, plans to retire in the spring and join her in North Carolina. They had planned to build a house. But their savings are mostly gone, Mrs. Perry said.

"The money has gone in so many different ways we didn't count on," she said. "When you get married, you think it's going to be you, your husband and your children. But it ends up being you, your husband, your children and both your parents."

Still, Martha Perry would not have it any other way. "It all goes back to slavery," she said. "Family was all anyone had."

Elder Care[2]

Making the Right Choice

BY JOHN GREENWALD
TIME, AUGUST 30, 1999

Marjorie Bryan's husband died 14 years ago. That was when she lived in Mississippi, and for some time afterward she went on living on her own. Now she's 82. A few years ago, she started having trouble with her balance and taking falls. Bryan has a grown son in Georgia, but moving in with him didn't seem like the answer. It's one thing to have a roof over your head. It's another to have a life. "I didn't want to live with my children," she says. "I think it would bore me to death. I don't drive anymore. If I'd stayed there, I'd be sort of a prisoner during the day."

So Bryan went looking at the alternatives. It turned out there were more than she had imagined. A couple of decades ago, seniors like her who were basically healthy but needed some assistance had limited choices. Among them, they could move in with their grown children, if they had any and were willing to risk the squabbling and sulking. Or they could be bundled off to a nursing home that was like a hospital, only less inviting. All that began to change in the early 1980s with the growth of a new range of living arrangements for older people who want to live as people, not patients, without the physical confinement and spiritual dead air of many nursing homes.

Eventually Bryan came upon the Gardens of Towne Lake in Woodstock, Ga., a landscaped complex where about two dozen seniors live in their own apartments and have round-the-clock staff members to help with daily tasks such as dressing and bathing. There are regular social events. There's a beauty shop. "I love living here," she says. "I got out that first day to learn names."

The late 20th century has done for the retirement years what it did for TV channels and fancy coffee. It multiplied the choices but also the consumer bewilderment. For seniors who want to stay in their homes as long as they can, there is home care for the masses—agencies everywhere that provide nurses and aides who either come by your place on a regular basis or live in. Traditional

---

nursing homes are still widely used, though they are evolving away from long-term care and toward rehabilitative facilities, for short-term stays following hospitalization. The most popular new options are assisted-living facilities. There are an estimated 20,000 to 30,000 such places in the U.S., according to industry figures. Assisted-living complexes are home to one-fourth of the 2.2 million Americans who live in housing for seniors, according to the American Seniors Housing Association. Some are free-standing facilities. Some are part of continuing-care retirement communities, which offer increasing levels of help and medical supervision as residents move through the years.

Assisted living gives the elderly some measure of independence, a chance to socialize and needed privacy.

"The assisted-living movement has really changed the way people age," says Karen Wayne, president of the Assisted Living Federation of America (ALFA), an industry trade group. "We've proved that people don't want to be in institutional settings." The facility provides each resident with a room or suite; meals, usually in a common dining room; and round-the-clock staff members who help with the no-big-deal chores of the day that can still defeat the mostly capable elderly—bathing, dressing, taking medication. Assisted living gives the elderly some measure of independence, a chance to socialize and needed privacy. Privacy for all sorts of things—sex has hardly disappeared from these seniors' lives. A survey released this month by the American Association of Retired Persons revealed that a quarter of those 75 or older say they have sex at least once a week.

The widening flood of Americans into later life—Tina Turner turns 60 this year!—guarantees that elder care will be a 21st century growth industry. The market, which was $86 billion in 1996, is expected to reach $490 billion by 2030. That potential is attracting such big developers as the Hyatt Corp. and Marriott International hotel operators. The 3,300 units of senior housing that Hyatt operates in 16 communities around the country are worth an estimated $500 million.

The old people that assisted living caters to are usually able to get out of bed and walk around. But their average age, estimated by ALFA, is 83, so they can also be frail. Almost half have Alzheimer's or some degree of cognitive impairment. (Alzheimer's patients tend to have their own, more closely supervised areas.) John Knox Village, in Pompano Beach, Fla., is a not-for-profit continuing-care operation on a landscaped campus with meandering walks and duck ponds. In an arrangement typical of such places, the elderly buy a residence—studio apartments are $48,500; two-bedroom "villas" are $142,500—and a continuing-care contract that sets a monthly maintenance fee covering all services. While they may begin life there in a mostly independent mode, taking an apartment with meals, they can later move to assisted-care rooms or even the on-campus nursing home for about the same monthly maintenance fee, usually a fraction of what a regular nursing home demands.

Carl Kielmann, 73, is a retired banker and the second generation of his family to live at John Knox in the Health Center. He and his wife Lillian moved there in 1985, joining his mother, who was also a resident. His mother's contract with Knox allowed her to spend her last six years in the village medical center without eating up her savings. "In a lot of ways," says Kielmann, "this type of place is your ultimate insurance policy."

Other assisted-care facilities can be a single building. Sunrise Assisted Living in Glen Cove, N.Y., is a 57,000-sq.-ft. soft yellow mansion with white gingerbread trimmings. The 83 seniors who live there each pay between $2,850 and $4,800 a month. On a recent day the buttery smell of fresh popcorn wafted through the vestibule. On the door of its suites, framed "memory boxes" display mementos of the lives of the people who live behind those doors—family photos, military dog tags and other souvenirs of long lives. In the special section for residents with Alzheimer's, one area is stocked with old tool kits, wedding gowns and a crib with several dolls, haunting but therapeutic props meant to engage the minds of people who have returned in fantasy to younger days when they worked and raised families. "We want to create pleasant days for these folks," says Jennifer Rehm, who runs the busy activity room. "This is not usually a neat place by the end of the day."

Keeping the elderly connected to the larger world is a big part of the idea behind assisted living. At the Munne Center in Miami, where family gatherings are featured, residents look forward to seeing their neighbors' grandchildren as eagerly as they do their own. Cecilia Struzzieri, 95, recently moved into Munne after living with her daughter. "I was getting feeble, and she wanted her freedom," Struzzieri says with a sigh. "Here I get all the attention I need." Miami developer Raul Munne, who built the place, is a Cuban immigrant. "Where I grew up," he jokes, "the elderly sat on the porch and fought with the neighborhood kids. It gave them incentive to get out of bed in the morning." But in the U.S., he says, "old folks are told, 'Don't open your door and go out at night. You might get mugged.' So, many of them have no one to talk to all day. They can only sit and watch television."

Later life lived this way doesn't come cheap. The Del Webb company, which made its name building luxury spas and retirement communities in the Sun Belt, last year opened a Sun City retirement community in Huntley, near frost-belted Chicago, an acknowledgment that seniors increasingly prefer to locate near longtime friends and family and not move to far-off sunny climes. Prices range from $130,000 for a single-level fourplex to $750,000 for customized estate homes that include home theaters, Jacuzzis and wine cellars, where an eminent Bordeaux can age along with its owners.

The typical assisted-living unit rents for about $2,000 a month, meals and basic services included. And prices can go much higher. Furthermore, assisted-living communities are not medical facilities, so their costs are not covered by Medicare or Medicaid, though 32 states do permit the limited use of Medicaid funds for assisted living. No wonder, then, that the average assisted-care resident has an income of $26,000 annually, while the typical retiree has $20,700.

The boomtown growth of the assisted-living industry has left it a bit rough around the edges. While nursing homes are federally regulated, assisted-living communities are overseen by the states and thus subject to widely varying standards. A federal study in four states (California, Florida, Ohio and Oregon) found "unclear or potentially misleading" language in sales brochures for about one-third of the 60 assisted-living homes surveyed. The most common problem was a failure to disclose the circumstances under which a resident can be expelled. One Florida home promised that seniors would not have to move if their health deteriorated, but the fine-print contract said physical or mental decline could be grounds for discharge.

Congress has begun poking into the problem, partly by way of its work to update the 1965 Older Americans Act, which provides penalties for scams on the elderly. "New services that meet the needs of our growing senior population are necessary and exciting," says Louisiana Senator John Breaux, ranking Democrat on the Senate Special Committee on Aging. "But the facilities are market driven and are susceptible to a bottom-line mentality that can lead to consumer fraud and abuse."

Of course, they are. Late-century American life is a social experiment in which we hope that market institutions can be fashioned to meet the most personal requirements. And sometimes they can be. New living arrangements for the elderly are still evolving. If that evolution isn't finished in time for all our parents to take advantage of, for many of us there will be a second chance—when it's our turn.

Seattle's Elderly Find a Home for Living, Not Dying[3]

By Sara Rimer
New York Times, November 22, 1998

It was Saturday night at the Providence-Mount St. Vincent nursing home. Marie Swegle, 96, and her friends on the fifth floor were lingering at the dinner table in their wheelchairs, watching the news. John Glenn had safely returned to Earth.

Mrs. Swegle, who a year before had learned to walk again after falling and breaking her neck, was not overly impressed by the 77-year-old astronaut. Neither was Effie Constantine, at 67 a good 15 years younger than anyone else at the table but crippled by hydrocephalus. "It's a waste of money, sending him up in space," she said. "Why don't they spend the money to study aging on earth?"

One place to start such a study might be at Providence-Mount St. Vincent, a five-story building surrounded by gardens at the top of a hill overlooking Elliott Bay. The Mount, as those who live there call it, is widely regarded to be what many Americans consider an impossibility: a good nursing home.

That is to say, in an industry freighted with the dread of old age, disability and loneliness, and periodically tainted by scandal and abuse, the Mount has found ways to be a home to people who can no longer care for themselves, to provide a sense of community in a place where no one wants to be, to be a community that is more about living than about dying.

The Mount is a place where Mrs. Swegle finds life sweet enough that she talks about wanting to make it to 100, where her friend down the hall, Vivian Grenfell, 83, who has a painful bone disease, looks forward to Fridays because that is when staff members help her put on her bathing suit and take her to a neighborhood pool so they can help her move her arms and legs in the water. Swimming is making her stronger.

---

3. Article by Sara Rimer from *New York Times,* November 22, 1999. Copyright © 1999 *New York Times.* Reprinted with permission.

Mrs. Grenfell, a retired dressmaker, belongs to a weekly ladies' luncheon group at the Mount, serves on the ethics committee and writes a column for its newspaper. Things were different at her first nursing home, she said: "You went in your room, you went in your bed. You didn't do much of anything."

As well as the Mount works, though, it cannot alter the stark realities of aging that its residents confront every day: the spouses, friends and even children outlived, the physical limitations, the loss of independence and control. These are men and women who survived the Depression, who fought in World War II, who worked as farmers, teachers, office managers, bus drivers and engineers, who raised families and ran houses, who now need help to go to the bathroom.

Each floor of the Mount is divided in half, one side nursing home, the other assisted-living apartments for less dependent residents. While some people come here, get well and return home, for most the Mount is the last address. "It's the end of the road," said 84-year-old Ruth Skoog, who grew up, graduated from high school, got married and raised a family in West Seattle at the bottom of the hill, and now, after two strokes, has arrived in Room 317 at the top.

The nursing home's population of 215 men and women is similar to that of most nursing homes: the sickest and most severely disabled elderly. The average age is 88. Eighty percent of the residents suffer from some degree of dementia.

When you are at the Mount, most of what staff members do day in and day out hardly seems extraordinary. The aides, nurses and social workers keep the residents clean and fed, take time to talk and to listen, and treat everyone —even the most demented—with respect and dignity. They enliven the atmosphere with the stuff of ordinary life: plants, pets, pictures on the wall, visits from children. This being Seattle, there is a coffee bar. The old enjoy a cup of latte, too.

"It's not rocket science," said Kevin Bail, a social worker who oversees the fifth floor. "It's basic stuff."

As nursing homes change and adapt under the pressure of managed care and Medicaid rules, even the visionary administrator behind the Mount, Robert Ogden, says it would be preferable for nursing homes to cease to exist—for people to be able to remain at home or in some other setting in their community. And alternatives are increasingly available.

But meanwhile, with nearly half of all Americans who reach 65 expected to spend time in a nursing home, health care professionals are looking to the Mount and a handful of places like it for answers.

Its current administrator, Charlene Boyd, says there is no reason the Mount cannot be duplicated. Money is a factor, she acknowledged; at about $60,000 a year, the Mount costs about $10,000 more than the national average. Yet half of its residents depend on Medicaid. Medicaid pays slightly less than the full rate. More important is breaking free of rigid rules and routines that assume residents are helpless.

But if the Mount is the last community for most of its residents, what is possible within a limited budget? How good can the end of the road be?

The Condition: Aging Residents Live with Pain and Loss

"I've got a dilapidating disease," Vivian Grenfell's roommate, Effie Constantine, was explaining to a visitor.

Mrs. Grenfell corrected her: "You mean debilitating."

"Right, debilitating—that sounds better," Mrs. Constantine said. "But I feel dilapidated."

They are all, in one way or another, debilitated and dilapidated, cut down by strokes, heart disease, Parkinson's, arthritis, osteoporosis, cancer, dementia and the sheer advance of time, dependent on Digoxin, Darvocet, Trazodone, Paxil, Tylenol and for calcium, nearly all of them, Tums. This is the condition that awaits anyone who lives long enough. And with the rapid growth in the 85-and-over population, it is a condition that increasing numbers of people will know. More than 1.5 million Americans live in nursing homes now.

> *More than 1.5 million Americans live in nursing homes now.*

Frances Mara was talking recently about how her father died of influenza in 1918, before he reached 40. Mrs. Mara, who spends her days alone in her room watching CNN, got her annual flu shot a few weeks ago. She is 84.

Though her hands are so bent and stiff from arthritis that she can no longer do the sewing she once enjoyed, a condition that no doubt contributes to her depression, Mrs. Mara never fails to vote, even if she needs help holding the pen to mark her absentee ballot. Voter turnout is high at the Mount.

But these survivors, many of them stoical in the face of enormous pain and loss, win no honor from a society that promotes longevity but at the same time denies death and shuns its emissaries, the frail elderly. "I see people back away from them when we go on trips," said Laurie Thode, a recreational coordinator.

They are not the active senior generation, the attractive silver-haired people celebrated in the media playing golf and going on cruises. The lucky ones among them are those who can walk, with walkers, and those who, as the residents put it, "have all their marbles."

It is easy to lump them together: a group of men and women in wheelchairs, a few staring vacantly, others nodding off. Even those who are fully aware are often unable, because of impairments, to show by expressions or gestures just how alive they are.

Ms. Thode and other staff members take pains to point out each individual. That 92-year old, the one moaning, "oh dear, oh dear," lived in a sod house in Alaska with her husband during World War II. The 81-year-old whose stroke left her struggling to utter a sentence? She once was an international toastmistress. The 83-year-old tethered to a feeding tube, who on some days doesn't know where he is, happens to be a much loved husband and father, who last week sat clutching a letter from his son, telling how his seventh-grade son had just gone to his first school dance with a girl.

"People ask me, how do you do this work day in and day out?" said Susan Scully, the social worker on the second floor. She tells them she enjoys the residents, and she means it—speaking as a social worker. "Things would be different," she said, "if they were my parents."

The Approach: Respect, Dignity Guide Care at the Mount

Monday morning: The weekly meeting of the third-floor residents was in session in the bird room, a cozy lounge with plush carpeting and big windows and an aviary.

Karla Heath, the registered nurse who oversees the floor, wanted to know if anyone had a complaint. How were the meals? Were they getting up in the morning when they wanted? What about the activities?

The finches were chirping away. The 11 people present— about a fourth of the floor—were mostly quiet, as usual. Rose Wilson, 81, did not breathe a word about the third-floor cat, Kit, who had singled out her bed for his afternoon naps; Mrs. Wilson hates cats.

It is not just that the residents are mostly pleased with the Mount, Ms. Heath would explain later. Most have already spent their savings to pay for their care, and are on Medicaid; those who are not will be in a matter of months. There is an underlying fear that if they complain, they might lose the last piece of security they have in the world: their beds here.

Some residents have come from other nursing homes, where they learned what it was like to wait 30 minutes or more for an aide to respond to a call button for a bathroom emergency. (At the Mount, aides must respond within three minutes.) "I just think they are very aware that they are dependent on others," Ms. Heath said.

Pressing on, Ms. Heath asked the group, "What about the food? Are you getting what you want? It's O.K. to ask for something different for breakfast."

Alice Berg, 90, who used to serve coffee and snacks on the state ferry to Vashon Island, volunteered that she had requested toast and orange juice that very morning. For Mrs. Berg, who daily proclaims her delight in every aspect of the Mount, it was an assertive step forward.

Lois Boppell, 87, who was born with cerebral palsy and had a job sorting bolts for Boeing, managed to get out, in her slurred speech, that she would like more fruit.

Lillian Reeder, 85, a retired elementary teacher with a bad heart, also had a request: "I would like more chopped up turkey, chicken and beef. It's easier to swallow."

Consider it done, Ms. Heath assured them.

She ended the meeting with a pep talk: "Everyone's going to go out there and speak up more for what they want, right?"

Seven years ago, the Mount was exactly the sort of place everyone dreaded.

"It was a very traditional nursing home—very institutional, very cold," said Mr. Ogden, who became the administrator in 1990.

The Mount's nursing home was opened by the Sisters of Providence in 1967, the beginning of a mass construction of nursing homes across the country financed by a new Federal health care program for the poor, Medicaid. For lack of any other model, these new institutions, something more than rest homes or old-age homes, were patterned after hospitals.

... the dramatic increase in longevity, combined with the transformation in society brought by increasing mobility and women going to work, meant a growing need for institutional care.

With Medicaid guaranteeing income, the care of the frail elderly became big business. And the dramatic increase in longevity, combined with the transformation in society brought by increasing mobility and women going to work, meant a growing need for institutional care.

"Nobody ever used to think of putting their grandparents in a nursing home," said Maureen Gladstone, 62, a nurse on the fifth floor whose grandmother lived with her family when she was growing up. "She helped raise us. Then when she got older, we took care of her."

In the old Mount, everything revolved around the staff members and their schedules. The day shift arrived at 6 A.M. and started getting everyone up for breakfast, whether they wanted to or not.

"We didn't know any better," said Mr. Ogden, who is now a regional director of long-term care and housing for the Sisters of Providence. "Our definition of care was to protect people to the point where they had no freedom, no dignity. We didn't want them to fall. We didn't want to be hurt by anything. The best thing we could think of to do was to put them away."

State regulators gave the Mount top ratings. That was how things worked in nursing homes, and how they still work in many.

As speculators and profiteers rushed into the business, conditions in the worst nursing homes led to scandals that helped shape Americans' fear of nursing homes. The scandals also prompted Congress to enact the 1987 Nursing Home Reform Law. Conditions slowly began to improve. Some health professionals began to talk about a new way of looking at nursing homes, one stressing the quality of residents' lives.

At the Mount, by then operated by the nonprofit Sisters of Providence Health System, Mr. Ogden and his assistant, Charlene Boyd, who has since succeeded him, began working with a team to carry out the new philosophy.

Each floor was divided into "neighborhoods" of about 20 residents each with their own dining room and kitchen. Anyone could get a snack or a cup of coffee at any time. White walls were painted pastel shades and hung with art. Floors were carpeted.

Residents were no longer automatically tied down at night in the name of protecting them. "The nurses came unglued," Mr. Ogden said. "They said the patients might fall out of bed. Some did. We picked them up and put them back. They slept better."

Medical diets calibrated down to the last gram of sugar and salt were thrown out or modified. "I went back to the docs and said, 'Does this really matter?'" Mr. Ogden said. "They said, 'No, not if you're 85.'"

Supervisory positions were eliminated and the money saved went to hire more aides. For all the innovations, for all the plants, pets and talk of vision, the success of the Mount comes down to the aides. They are the ones who spend the most time with the residents, bathing, dressing, feeding, changing and talking with them.

At night, Ruth Skoog turns to her aide, Gloria Alderman, for comfort. "I say, 'Gloria sing me a song; I don't feel so good,'" Mrs. Skoog said the other evening as Ms. Alderman, who is a gospel singer, fed her a dinner of pureed food, a necessity because of Mrs. Skoog's bowel problems.

In another nursing home, Mrs. Skoog might be classified as a "feeder." To Ms. Alderman and the other aides, Mrs. Skoog is a beauty queen; they all know she won the Miss West Seattle crown when she was 18, and they see to it that her nails are manicured and her lipstick is fresh.

Aides at most nursing homes are paid little more than minimum wage. The Mount pays about $10 an hour. But pay is just part of the difference. Aides are trained in what the Mount calls "resident-directed care"—what it means, how to make it work, why the Mount believes in it.

Every aide is part of a team that cares for a specific group of residents. Other staff members, including nurses and social workers, help them when they need help. And aides are recognized throughout the year with gifts, special days and opportunities to attend professional conferences. There is turnover—about 30 percent a year—but the average nursing home has 100 percent.

Many of the aides are from Africa and Southeast Asia. They all comment that they never saw a nursing home until they came to America.

"We don't have these kinds of facilities," said Tesfaye Begosa, who is from Ethiopia. "Whenever your parents get old, you just take them to your place."

The Unconventional: Mixing Residents to End Hierarchy

Everyone predicted disaster when Mr. Ogden decided to unlock the 56-bed Alzheimer's ward on the fourth floor and mix its residents with everyone else.

"Eighty percent of the social workers walked out," said one aide, Tamara Allen, who vehemently opposed the move but now is so sold on the change that she gives speeches about it at conferences. "We just couldn't imagine how it would be."

That there were problems with the old way, she could not deny. In her trademark speech, she describes the caste system that still operates in many nursing homes: "Independent residents look down on the residents that need help, and they in turn look down on the residents who are confused."

Maureen Gladstone, the nurse, recalled the fears of "the alerts and non-agitateds"—jargon for those without dementia. "I asked them, 'What is it about them that bothers you?'" she said. "They were afraid they'd be that way. It's like a mirror."

But chaos did not erupt. On the contrary, Alzheimer's patients became less agitated. When those who seemed likely to wander off were fitted with ankle bracelets that would signal when they were leaving, and through which door, "They didn't seem to roam around," Ms. Gladstone said. "Just the idea that they could go wherever they wanted—they didn't want to anymore."

Unlocking the fourth floor was an effort to eliminate the hierarchy that defines most nursing homes, where floors are organized by disability and impairment, forcing frail elderly people who have already given up their homes and their communities to move again as they decline.

"Everyone was terrified of moving to the fourth floor," Ms. Boyd said.

A Dilemma: Balancing a Range of People's Needs

Vivian Grenfell and Marie Swegle were having dinner with five other residents at their regular table on the fifth floor. The conversation turned to a recent outing to the new Nordstrom's downtown.

"I am not exaggerating, it's the most beautiful store I've ever seen," said Mrs. Swegle, who taught elementary school before she was married, attends mass daily in the Mount's chapel and manages to look regal in her neck brace and collar, accessorized with a string of pearls. "I saw a hat I liked. It had a turned-up brim, and a little bit of red in it. My better sense told me I was getting too old to buy it."

Another woman at the table, who has Alzheimer's, was focused on the corn on her plate. "I just love corn," she repeated several times, with a radiant smile.

"She fits in beautifully," Effie Constantine had said earlier of her tablemate.

At another table, a woman with dementia whose tendency toward foul language has made her something of an outcast was crying out: "Help, I can't walk! Don't undress me! Help!"

"I feel I'm very inadequate," she said imploringly to Tamara Allen, the aide.

Mrs. Allen put her arm around her and stroked her hair. "You're not," she said. "You're fine."

Listened to night after night, the ravings of the unmoored have become the background noise of the fifth floor, like the television that is sometimes left on. Much of it, fortunately, is lost on those residents who are hard of hearing.

"I think it's a good thing they mixed in the Alzheimer's people," Mrs. Swegle volunteered. She recalled a visit she made to the old locked fourth floor. "I went up to see a friend of mine," she said. "It frightened me. One woman came at me with a stick. It's because they had been shut up together for so long. I think it got on their nerves. It's better to be out."

"One of my neighbors came down with Alzheimer's," she added. "She's here. I see her every once in a while. She makes very sensible remarks."

Things have been more difficult on the third floor, where 87-year-old Maxine Christian's dementia causes her to moan and cry out continually.

"What am I going to do about Maxine?" Ms. Heath said the other day in exasperation. She had tried changes in medication, lab tests that might detect a physical problem, music, a rocking chair, art projects with a recreational coordinator, Niki Hopkins.

Ms. Heath had spent hours trying to comfort Mrs. Christian. "What's wrong, Maxine?" she had asked her, over and over. Mrs. Christian, a former artist who can no longer paint, and whose son died of leukemia at age 45, never had an answer.

Ms. Heath said she wished she could give Mrs. Christian a private room, in part to spare her roommate, but private rooms are few and hard to come by at the Mount. In an ideal world, she said, everyone in a nursing home could have a private room.

Now Ms. Heath had summoned Mrs. Christian's husband of 60 years, Ed. Seated at a table in her office, the 86-year-old retired electrician wept as she told him she had to think of the 40 other residents on the floor. "She's disrupting the community," she said. When it comes to Mrs. Christian, apparently, the residents are not shy about complaining. "They're all saying, 'Can't you do something?'"

"Is she the worst one you've ever had?" he asked.

The answer was no. Ms. Heath, her own eyes watering, put her hand on his arm.

A week or so later, with still no improvement, Ms. Heath said one solution, which she was not crazy about, might be to increase Mrs. Christian's anti-anxiety medication. She did not want to consider the other alternative, discharging Mrs. Christian and leaving her husband to find another nursing home. "We're just going to have to make it work," she said.

The Adjustment: A New Life, with Ups and Downs

Adjusting to a nursing home can be more difficult for those who are not demented.

Six months ago Ruth Skoog, a former freelance writer for *The Seattle Times,* had an apartment of her own in the assisted-living half of the Mount. She was a big wheel, serving on the all-important food committee and the residents council and joining all the organized outings. Then back-to-back strokes partly paralyzed her and she crossed the hall into the nursing home.

The other evening Mrs. Skoog was at dinner on the third floor. "She's got all her marbles," she said, paying the ultimate compliment to the woman in the wheelchair beside her, Ann Hasslinger, a former marathon runner who, at a youthful 43, has advanced multiple sclerosis.

Adjusting to a nursing home can be more difficult for those who are not demented.

The same could not be said of many of the women, in their 80s and 90s, around them. "This is appalling," Mrs. Skoog said. "If my husband could see me now, he would die. He hated to visit his own mother in the nursing home."

Mrs. Skoog wishes there were more people she could talk to, and yet she carries on. She questions aides closely about life outside the Mount. Ms. Heath even says her complaining is a sign of health.

As the former Miss West Seattle went off in her wheelchair for her weekly hair appointment, she said, "One has to keep up one's image."

Nursing homes look different to people depending on their age, their health, their stage of life. In their 70s, Dick and Esther Gorman made a pledge: No nursing homes. But when the couple turned 80 together, they began down a path that would lead them to an assisted-living apartment at the Mount—and the understanding that someday they might move across the corridor, to the nursing home.

In a letter sent to all their friends, Mr. Gorman related why they began searching for a final home and what they learned. Their health, "while very good was starting to show signs of changes typical of 80-year-olds," he wrote. "Although we were quite sound organically, it had become apparent we were experiencing some memory loss, loss of energy, occasional confusion."

Visiting retirement communities and assisted-living facilities, including the Mount, "we found each had its share of quite disabled people and that frequently they would be sitting (sometimes sprawled out and/or asleep) in the lobby. This was culture shock for us, seeing all these old people."

They decided not to move until they absolutely had to— but soon they reconsidered. Looking at themselves more closely, he wrote, "we began to see that we weren't that far away from being those old people whose presence upset us." In June 1997 they moved to the Mount.

Since then, 18 residents they knew have died. "There's a sort of unspoken agreement among people who are here that mortality is real, but nothing to worry about," said Mr. Gorman, the president of the assisted-living residents council. "You have to consider that a part of living is deteriorating."

And now that he makes regular visits to the nursing home to visit friends, including Mrs. Skoog, he says it no longer holds the horror that it once did. "We're all heading in that direction," he said.

Nursing homes look different to people depending on their age, their health, their stage of life.

The death notices go up in the corridors every few days, it seems. In the first week of November, four residents died.

The last, 91-year-old Mildred Burke, was the day's featured obituary in *The Seattle Times*. Ms. Burke had helped develop smaller hearing aids and voice boxes, had been a crack swimmer, sailor and skier, and had volunteered her time to visit hundreds of people in nursing homes before entering one herself.

But death is not what people at the Mount fear most. For all the fears that Americans have of nursing homes, like soldiers in battle the aged fear a crippling disability more than death. They are way past American society's illusion that youth is eternal.

"Am I going to be bedridden?" said Vivian Grenfell, who hopes her weekly sessions in a pool will help ward off that day. "Is that the next step?"

Soren Dahl, 85, says he considers himself lucky to have landed the bed by the window in Room 563. He has a spectacular view of Puget Sound, downtown Seattle and, beyond, the mountains.

Mr. Dahl spends hours at the window, tracking planes, ferries, lights at night. He invites visitors to sit and watch with him.

How did he get the room with the view? The previous occupant, Mr. Dahl said matter-of-factly, died.

Better, Safer, Warmer[4]

By Cynthia Kaplan
New York Times, February 1, 1999

It happened very suddenly and was perhaps the most violent act in which I have ever participated. A space became available and we had to grab it or risk waiting maybe six or eight months for another.

I don't know why I thought there would be more warning. It's not as if they call you up and say we're expecting Mrs. Feingold to sign off in about two months so you should start to get ready. Mrs. Feingold or whoever just dies and they clean up her room and they call you. That's it.

So my parents and I packed up my grandmother's winter clothing, a few pictures and books and some of her music, and tore her out of the ground like a mandrake root. And although she came willingly, the silent scream was there, not so silent; I could hear it. We all could.

Despite our best efforts to prepare her, there was no way she could have known what was happening. And despite our best intentions, here is what was happening: Come, put on your coat, get in the car, you will never see this place, your home, again. Sorry, sorry, sorry.

At first she was excited. She was finally out of the apartment, out and on her way to, where? Well, to the good new place, we said. To the place near Mom and Dad. With a piano. None of us could say nursing home.

But then, after half an hour in the car, she stopped wanting information and started wanting soup. When we got to The Place everyone gave my grandmother the big welcome. They gave her soup. They gave us all soup. We walked her around the common rooms and gardens, which were beautiful. Nurses and aides and administrators made a fuss over her, which she loves. She was bubbly and charming and spoke nonsense and everyone thought she was adorable. My parents and I made furtive eye contact; it was going so well, but still, all I could think was: Just wait.

We went to her room or, rather, her half room. It was small and the wallpaper was a psychedelic flower pattern that it seemed to me could itself induce dementia. The furniture was old and the bed creaky and hospital-like. I went out into the hall and cried.

There was a roommate who was incensed to find people in her room. We drew the curtains that divided the space. At least my grandmother had the window half, looking out onto the gardens. At least, at least. She had not shared a room with anyone besides her husband in 70 years. Now she was going to share it with a mean stranger. I went into the hall again and cried. My grandmother was taken off for an evaluation of some kind. We waited in her room in a state of what can only be described as wistful dread. Surely the other shoe was going to drop.

It did. My grandmother returned distraught, furious. She hates to be poked and prodded and questioned, and she was ready to go home. She said: Get me out of here. You have to take me out of here. I've had enough. You can just kill me if you want, but I won't stay here. I'll just lie down on the floor. That's all. I'll just lie down on the floor and die.

Now we had to explain to her why she wasn't going home, why she had to stay tonight, and maybe for a while. We didn't mention forever; what a ridiculous, damaging concept that is. My father left the room for a few minutes, maybe to figure out what would be the best thing to say, maybe to cry. While he was gone the roommate poked her head through the curtain and said, It's a nice place, really. But my grandmother was inconsolable.

My father came back and said quietly, Mom, you have to stay. That was it for me, and I went back out into the hall.

As I write this, my grandmother has been there two weeks. At least one of us has seen her every day, even though she doesn't always know who we are and will probably not remember that we were there. We walk with her in the garden. We sit and people-watch. We talk her into playing the piano in the lobby. (She complains that it is not as nice as hers, and she's right.)

We have endless conversations with her aide and nurse and social worker so they'll know what she likes and doesn't like, who she is, so they'll understand her. My brother has come with his children, and even my mother-in-law, way above and beyond the call of duty, has visited.

She is still very confused by her surroundings, calls everyone names behind their backs (actually, she barely waits until they are out of view, much less out of earshot) and thinks the social worker is someone she knows from the beach. Sometimes when we arrive she seems all right, sometimes she collapses into our arms, lost and distraught.

Each day she takes her clothes out of the drawers and the closet, folds them beautifully and packs what she can into the small straw bag I brought for her piano music, then leaves the rest piled on the bed and dresser. She carries her pocketbook everywhere and sometimes tries to go out the emergency door. She talks incessantly of going home (who wouldn't?), of getting on the train she sometimes hears in the distance and going back to her apartment.

This will change, we know. In time she will make friends and have activities. (O.K., she'll never have activities; she hates activities.) She will be cared for around the clock by people who are trained to meet the needs of people with Alzheimer's. We tell her: Stay for now, stay for the winter, it's better, safer, warmer, closer, whatever. We tell her what we hope she'll understand.

But she is planning a break-out, I think. Dear Sarah, (Who?) Send help. I need help. Help please. She has written this on a paper towel and put it in her pocketbook. She is our hostage. As I said, it feels like the most violent act in which I have ever participated. I would take it back, if I could.

IV. Perceptions of
Aging in America

Editor's Introduction

How the elderly are perceived in America was among the aspects of aging that interested me most as I undertook the editing of this book. Yet there were few articles that addressed this topic in popular magazines and journals. It is an issue relegated largely to professional and academic publications aimed at sociologists, social workers, psychologists, and gerontologists. The selections here are intended as a starting point, to stimulate thinking about this complex social topic. Most discussions aimed at general audiences took the form of books, and so I have included portions of two of them here.

Although the title of this book is *Aging in America*, I felt it would be useful to briefly address aging in other cultures, if only to point out that there are ways of perceiving the aged that differ drastically from our own. In "Sage or Spoilsport?" (*The UNESCO Courier*) by Bernadette Puijalon and Jacqueline Trincaz, the writers contrast perceptions of aging in traditional rural cultures in Africa with those in Western societies. Far from being looked on as a burden, or as no longer useful, in Africa the oldest members of a community are typically its most revered, for they are seen as having amassed knowledge and wisdom throughout their lifetimes that are vital to the group.

In the first chapter of *Successful Aging*, John W. Rowe and Robert L. Kahn refute some of Americans' most deeply held assumptions about what it means to grow old. One by one, they address six myths related to aging—"You Can't Teach an Old Dog New Tricks," for example—and proceed to debunk them based on scientific evidence gathered over the course of 10 years as part of the MacArthur Foundation Study of Successful Aging. According to the book's foreword, the study "assembled a group of scholars from major disciplines relevant to aging to develop the conceptual basis of a 'new gerontology.' The project: Conduct a long-term research program to gather the knowledge needed to improve older Americans' physical and mental abilities." The study's overall findings prove strikingly that successful aging is well within reach for the vast majority of Americans. While the writers admit that uprooting the negative myths surrounding aging may be difficult, they contend "Acknowledging the truth about aging in America is critical . . . if we are to move ahead toward successful aging as individuals and as a society."

Mary Pipher is a clinical psychologist and the author of *The Shelter of Each Other*, a discussion of American families; and most notably, *Reviving Ophelia*, her best-selling book about teenage girls. In *Another Country—Navigating the Emotional Terrain of Our Elders*, she tackles the subject of aging, contending that Americans must attempt to overcome the generation gaps and fears of old age and death that lead us to segregate our society according to age. Focusing on baby boomers and their parents, the latter of whom make up America's current older population, the book deals specifically with some of the differences in values, upbringing, and outlook that exist between these generations; the conflicts these differences may cause; and ways to help overcome them. In this excerpt, culled from chapters one and two of her book, she gives an overview of some of these fears and generational differences, showing how they precipitate our society's treatment and perceptions of the elderly and the lack of connection that often exists between young and old. She also briefly contrasts our treatment of older people with the treatment they receive in other cultures, and addresses the hurdles we face in coping with the difficulties of aging in contemporary America, where often families are dispersed and lives are hectic. "Aging in America," Pipher writes, "is harder than it needs to be."

Sage or spoilsport?[1]

In Africa the aged are the guardians of knowledge and power; in the West they are all too often regarded as an encumbrance

BY BERNADETTE PUIJALON AND JACQUELINE TRINCAZ
THE UNESCO COURIER, JANUARY 1999

Old age is as much a historical and cultural construct as a natural phenomenon. It is based on biological, demographic, economic and political factors, but it is also built on the image of old age—in some cases positive, in others less so—that each society shapes in conformity with its values and its conception of what constitutes an ideal human being.

Some cultures have emphasized the positive side of growing old by viewing human development as a lifelong process in which the aging individual accumulates qualities and experiences. One example of this can be found in the traditional rural societies of Africa, where social differentiation is based on age, which establishes the superiority of the older over the younger generation. In these societies the elderly are few in number but they play a big role.

In these systems where the oral tradition prevails, knowledge is the property of the very old—not so much technical knowledge, which anyone can soon absorb, as "mythical knowledge" that no young person can take away from them. Those who possess the secret of the sacred myth that describes the group's origins, know the profound meaning of things and the Law of the Ancestors, in other words the principle that governs and regulates the social order. Myth engenders ritual, the repetition of the primordial gesture, making the elderly the officiants of the domestic cult, capable of uttering sacred words, unleashing vital good or evil powers and issuing blessings and curses.

The elderly have a vitally important educational role because of their mastery of knowledge. As well as telling young generations about myth, they must transmit the history of the group and its social rules, of which they are the guardians. Transmission takes place in stages, especially during the initiation ceremonies which

---

1. Article by Bernadette Puijalon and Jacqueline Trincaz from *The Unesco Courier*, January 1999. Copyright © 1999 *The Unesco Courier*. Reprinted with permission.

are milestones in the education process, enabling the elderly to keep part of the secret knowledge as long as possible and guaranteeing their cultural, religious and political hegemony. Gerontocratic power is rooted in this system. "The process is simple," says French anthropologist Louis Vincent Thomas. It consists of "confiscating basic knowledge, then serving it to the rising age groups in precisely measured doses at well-calculated intervals through a language rich in symbols and highly emotional resonances."

Benefactions from beyond the Grave

Aging is thus a process of acquisition, and the image of the elderly is highly positive. An old man is wise. He sets an example and has cheated death by drawing inspiration from the group's values. He does not fear death, which will reunite him with his ancestors and enable him to continue being useful to the community by eternally making benefactions to his descendants.

Envisaging life as an ongoing progression that continues after death leads to a conception of old age as the last stage of an ascension towards fullness of knowledge and power.

What Western societies call loss of faculties, disability and degeneration are symptoms of a metamorphosis towards a higher stage. If an old person can't keep to the point, perhaps he is talking with the ancestors. If he goes blind or deaf, he is seeing and listening to the spirits. If he shrivels up and finds it hard to get about, he has become a spirit. Accomplished, close to God and the ancestors, he lives as one of the elect. In such a society people enjoy aging and saying they are old—even very, very old. The term has many positive associations. Adding "wise" would be redundant.

The Quest for Eternal Youth

Western societies, on the other hand, divide the human life span into successive periods in which phases of growth, maturity and climax are followed by decline and fall, leading to the inevitable, irreversible end. Faced with the unprecedented increase in life expectancy and the ever-growing number of elderly persons, these societies have two watchwords: individual resistance to aging and the solidarity of all with the poorest elderly people.

Since old age is neither desirable nor enviable, people should try and delay its onset as long as possible. They have no right to squander their capital of youthfulness; they must resist the ravages of time by leading healthy lives and taking advantage of all the remedies science has to offer—pills, health creams or surgery. The purpose of preventive action against old age is not to develop a person's capacities for living but to reject this stage of life because it is viewed as degrading.

This struggle is a matter of individual responsibility and the "losers"—those who fail to stay young in mind and body when they fall ill, suffer bereavement or have an accident—feel guilty. For them, life has taken a sudden, drastic turn. They have entered old age, the age of dependence. The criterion upon which this transition is based is not social or cultural but biological. It depends on an individual's physical capacities rather than on his or her chronological age. In Western societies this time of life is dominated by negative images—loneliness, incapacity and social uselessness.

Caring is the key word. When old age is synonymous with inadequacy and decline, certain things have to be done. Social workers specializing in geriatric care use special assessment methods to decide what kind of assistance should be given and what resources should be used, from geriatric medicine to long-term care facilities. This process has a logic of its own and raises the question of the cost of dependence, which strengthens the overwhelming image of the elderly as an economic burden. Never, perhaps, has a society done so much for its oldest members. They benefit from economic and social protection, but the image society has of them is deeply negative.

Segregation between Age Groups

Historians have shown that a society's image of individuals at a given stage of life has a significant bearing on the way they are treated. Paradoxically, Western societies, where there are more and more elderly people, organize an unprecedented form of segregation between the age groups. Young and old pursue different activities in different places at different times. The harmonious mingling of the ages in a shared setting no longer exists.

In Africa, the transformation of the traditional context by such processes as urbanization, schooling and the development of a culture based on the written word, the intermingling of populations, the spread of new religions and the arrival of new, more individualistic values are diluting if not destroying the community system and gerontocracy. Knowledge and power have changed hands. Those societies may be witnessing the "twilight of the old." However, no society remains frozen. And even when the age pyramid is turned upside down—when more people start appearing at the top than at the bottom, as in the West or in some Asian countries that have implemented proactive birth control policies—solidarity may still have a role to play—but only if a process of give-and-take between generations is restored to human relationships.

Breaking Down the Myths of Aging[2]

BY JOHN W. ROWE, M.D., AND ROBERT L. KAHN, PH.D.
EXCERPT FROM THE BOOK *SUCCESSFUL AGING*

The topic of aging is durably encapsulated in a layer of myths in our society. And, like most myths, the ones about aging include a confusing blend of truth and fancy. We have compressed six of the most familiar of the aging myths into single-sentence assertions—frequently heard, usually with some link to reality, but always (thankfully) in significant conflict with recent scientific data.

MYTH #1: To be old is to be sick.
MYTH #2: You can't teach an old dog new tricks.
MYTH #3: The horse is out of the barn.
MYTH #4: The secret to successful aging is to choose your parents wisely.
MYTH #5: The lights may be on, but the voltage is low.
MYTH #6: The elderly don't pull their own weight.

Contrasting these myths with scientific fact leads to the conclusion that our society is in persistent denial of some important truths about aging. Our perceptions about the elderly fail to keep pace with the dramatic changes in their actual status. We view the aged as sick, demented, frail, weak, disabled, powerless, sexless, passive, alone, unhappy, and unable to learn—in short, a rapidly growing mass of irreversibly ill, irretrievable older Americans. To sum up, the elderly are depicted as a figurative ball and chain holding back an otherwise spry collective society. While this image is far from true, evidence that the bias persists is everywhere around us. Media attention to the elderly continues to be focused on their frailty, occasionally interspersed, in recent years, by equally unrealistic presentations of improbably youthful elders. Gerontologists, an important group of scholars which has become prominent during the last few decades, have been as much a part of the problem as the solution. Their literature has been preoccupied with concerns about frailty, nursing home admissions, and the social and health care needs of multiply impaired elders.

---

2. Excerpted from *Successful Aging* by John Wallis Rowe and Robert L. Kahn. Copyright ©1998 by John Wallis Rowe, M.D., and Robert L. Kahn, Ph.D. Reprinted with permission.

That we as a society are obsessed with the negative rather than the positive aspect of aging is not a new observation. Robert Butler, a pioneering gerontologist and geriatrician who was founding director of the National Institute on Aging and established the United States' first formal Department of Geriatric Medicine at Mount Sinai Medical Center in New York, coined the term "ageism" in his Pulitzer Prize-winning book *Growing Old in America—Why Survive?* in 1975. Butler saw ageism as similar to racism and sexism—a negative view of a group, and a view divorced from reality. More recently Betty Friedan, a leading architect of the women's movement, wrote about the mystique that surrounds aging in America, and our obsession with "the problem of aging." The persistence of the negative, mythic view of older persons as an unproductive burden has been underlined in recent congressional debates as to

> *The persistence of the negative, mythic view of older persons as an unproductive burden has been underlined in recent congressional debates as to whether America can "afford the elderly."*

whether America can "afford the elderly." Ken Dychtwald, founder and CEO of Age Wave, Inc., has consistently sounded the call for a realistic view of aging and of older persons, exhorting American corporations to become more responsive to elders' needs.

Most of us resist replacing myth-based beliefs with science-based conclusions. It involves letting go of something previously ingrained in order to make way for the newly demonstrated facts. Learning something new requires "unlearning" something old and perhaps deeply rooted. Acknowledging the truth about aging in America is critical, however, if we are to move ahead toward successful aging as individuals and as a society. In order to make use of the new scientific knowledge and experience its benefits in our daily lives, we must first "unlearn" the myths of aging. Here we present each myth with a glimpse of the scientific evidence that corrects or contradicts it. In the following chapters of this book, we will explore that evidence in greater detail and discover its implications for how long, and how well, we live.

MYTH #1: "To Be Old Is to Be Sick"

Ironically, myth #1 could be the title of many a gerontological text. Happily, though, the MacArthur Study and other important research has proved the statement false. Still, a central question regarding the status of the elderly is, "Just who is this new breed of seniors?" Are we facing an increased number of very sick old people, or is the new elder population healthier and more robust?

The first clue comes in the prevalence of diseases. Throughout the century there has been a shift in the patterns of sickness in the aging population. In the past, acute, infectious illness dominated. Today, chronic illnesses are far more prevalent. The most common ailments in today's elderly include the following: arthritis (which affects nearly half of all old people), hypertension and heart disease (which affect nearly a third), diabetes (11 percent), and disorders which influence communication such as hearing impairment (32 percent), cataracts (17 percent), and other forms of visual impairments including macular degeneration (9 percent). When you compare sixty-five- to seventy-four-year-old individuals in 1960 with those similarly aged in 1990, you find a dramatic reduction in the prevalence of three important precursors to chronic disease: high blood pressure, high cholesterol levels, and smoking. We also know that between 1982 and 1989, there were significant reductions in the prevalence of arthritis, arteriosclerosis (hardening of the arteries), dementia, hypertension, stroke and emphysema (chronic lung disease), as well as a dramatic decrease in the average number of diseases an older person has. And dental health has improved as well. The proportion of older individuals with dental disease so severe as to result in their having no teeth has dropped from 55 percent in 1957 to 34 percent in 1980, and is currently approaching 20 percent.

But what really matters is not the number or type of diseases one has, but how those problems impact on one's ability to function. For instance, if you are told that a white male is age seventy-five, your ability to predict his functional status is limited. Even if you are given details of his medical history, and learn he has a history of hypertension, diabetes, and has had a heart attack in the past, you still couldn't say whether he is sitting on the Supreme Court of the United States or in a nursing home!

There are two key ways to determine people's ability to remain independent. One is to assess their ability to manage their personal care. The personal care activities include basic functions, such as dressing, bathing, toileting, feeding oneself, transferring from bed to chair, and walking. The second category of activities is known as nonpersonal care. These are tasks such as preparing meals, shopping, paying bills, using the telephone, cleaning the house, writing, and reading. A person is disabled or dependent when he or she cannot perform some of these usual activities without assistance. When you look at sixty-five-year-old American men, who have a total life expectancy of fifteen more years, the picture is a surprisingly positive one: twelve years are likely to be spent fully independent. By age eighty-five, the picture is more bleak: nearly half of the future years are spent inactive or dependent.

Life expectancy for women is substantially greater than that for men. At age sixty-five, women have almost nineteen years to live—four more than men of the same age. And for women, almost fourteen of those will be active, and five years dependent.

It is important to recognize that this dependency is not purely a function of physical impairments but represents, particularly in

---

When you look at sixty-five-year-old American men, who have a total life expectancy of fifteen more years, the picture is a surprisingly positive one: twelve years are likely to be spent fully independent.

---

advanced age, a mixture of physical and cognitive impairment. Even at age eighty-five, women have a life expectancy advantage nearly one and a half years over men and are likely to spend about half of the rest of their lives independent.

There are two general schools of thought regarding the implications of increased life expectancy on the overall health status of the aging population. One holds that the same advances in medical technology will produce not only longer life, but also less disease and disability in old age. This optimistic theory predicts a reduction in the incidence of nonfatal disorders such as arthritis, dementia, healing impairment, diabetes, hypertension, and the like. It is known as the "compression of morbidity" theory—in a nutshell, it envisions prolonged active life and delayed disability for older people. A contrasting theory maintains just the opposite: that our population will become both older and sicker.

The optimistic theory may be likened to the tale of the "one horse shay" by Oliver Wendell Holmes. Some sixty-five to seventy years ago, when one of us (RLK) was reluctantly attending the Fairbanks Elementary School in Detroit, students were required to memorize poetry. One of Robert's favorites was a long set of verse by Oliver Wendell Holmes entitled "The Deacon's Masterpiece or The Wonderful One-Horse Shay." (A shay was a two-wheeled buggy, usually fitted with a folding top. The word itself, shay, is a New England adaptation from the French *chaise.*)

The relevance of all this to gerontology becomes clear early in the poem. The deacon was exasperated with the tendency of horse-drawn carriages to wear out irregularly; one part or another would fail when the rest of the vehicle was still in prime condition. He promised to build a shay in which every part was equally strong and durable, so that it would not be subject to the usual break-downs of one or another part. And he was marvelously successful. The shay showed no sign of aging whatsoever until the first day of its 101st year, when it suddenly, instantly, and mysteriously turned to dust. The poem concludes with a line that stays in memory after all the intervening years. It is the poet's challenge to those who find the story difficult to believe. Since every part of the shay was equally durable, collapse of all had to come at the same moment: "End of the wonderful one-hoss shay; logic is logic; that's all I say."

MacArthur Studies and other research show us that older people are much more likely to age well than to become decrepit and dependent.

The second, more negative theory—in which older people become sicker and more dependent with increasing age—is losing favor. MacArthur Studies and other research show us that older people are much more likely to age well than to become decrepit and dependent. The fact is, relatively few elderly people live in nursing homes. Only 5.2 percent of older people reside in such institutions, a figure which declined significantly from the 6.3 percent found in a 1982 survey. Furthermore, most older Americans are free of disabilities. Of those aged sixty-five to seventy-four in 1994, a full 89 percent report no disability whatsoever. While the proportion of elderly who are fully functioning and robust declines with advancing age, between the age of seventy-five to eighty-four, 73 percent still report no disability, and even after age eighty-five, 40 percent of the population is fully functional.

Between 1982 and 1994, the proportion of the population over age sixty-five that reported any disability fell from 24.9 percent to 21.3 percent, a meaningful reduction. And another statistic really sends the message home: in the United States today there are 1.4 million fewer disabled older people than there would be had the status of the elderly not improved since 1982. Furthermore, many studies show that the reduction in disability among older people appears to be accelerating. This is true at all ages, even among those over age ninety-five.

And so, the optimistic vision of aging seems to hold true—and the fact that the elderly population is relatively healthy and independent bears on the future of social policies for older people. It has important implications for issues as broad as establishing the proper eligibility age for Social Security benefits, and projecting the likely future expenses of federal health care programs including Medicare and Medicaid. Furthermore, beyond social policy implications, the greater our understanding of disability trends, the greater, in turn will be our insights into the degree of biological change in our aging population. Disability in older people results from three key factors 1) the impact of disease, or more commonly, many diseases at once; 2) lifestyle factors, such as exercise and diet, which directly influence physical fitness and risk of disease; and 3) the biological changes that occur with advancing age—formally

---

. . . beyond social policy implications, the greater our understanding of disability trends, the greater, in turn will be our insights into the degree of biological change in our aging population.

---

known as senescence. It is not clear whether the reduction in the incidence of many chronic diseases—and the reduction in many risk factors for those diseases—is connected to a more general slowdown in the rate of physical aging. There is increasing evidence that the rate of physical aging is not as we once believed, determined by genes alone. Lifestyle factors—which can be changed—have powerful influence as well. We will discuss this in much greater detail later in the book, but it's a very empowering notion to keep in mind. We can, and should, take some responsibility for the way in which we grow older.

So far, we have been focusing on objective information about older people's ability to function. But another important issue is how older people *perceive* their own health status. Again, we are optimistic. Research finds that older people have a quite positive view of their own health. In one major study, older people were asked to rate their health as excellent, very good, good, fair, or poor. In 1994, 39 percent of individuals over the age of sixty-five viewed their health as very good or excellent, while only 29 percent considered their health to be fair or poor. Even among those over age eighty-five, 31 percent considered themselves to be in very good or excellent health, while 36 percent viewed themselves as in poor health. Men and women were equally positive, but there were some racial differences—for instance, older African Americans were more likely than Caucasians to rate their health as poor. In general, however, a growing body of evidence shows that older people perceive themselves as healthy, even in the face of real physical problems. Why the occasional dissonance between objective measures of health and people's perceptions of it? It may reflect a remarkably successful adaptation to disability. Despite society's view of older persons as frail and in poor health, older people simply don't share that view, even when they have objective evidence of disability.

In sum, decades of research clearly debunk the myth that to be old in America is to be sick and frail. Older Americans are generally healthy. Even in advanced old age, an overwhelming majority of the elderly population have little functional disability, and the proportion that is disabled is being whittled away over time. We are delighted to observe increasing momentum toward the emergence of a physically and cognitively fit, nondisabled, active elderly population. The combination of longer life and less illness is adding life to years as well as years to life.

The combination of longer life and less illness is adding life to years as well as years to life.

At the same time, as a result of the MacArthur Foundation Studies of Aging in America and other research, we now can identify the lifestyle and personality factors that boost the chance of aging successfully. This book discusses strategies to reduce one's risk of disease and disability, and to maintain physical and mental function. Our main message is that we can have a dramatic impact on our own success or failure in aging. Far more than is usually assumed, successful aging is in our own hands. What we can do for ourselves, however, depends partly on the opportunities and constraints that are presented to us as we age—in short, on the attitudes and expectations of others toward older people, and on policies of the larger society of which we are a part.

MYTH # 2: "You Can't Teach an Old Dog New Tricks"

The pervasive belief among young and old that the elderly cannot sharpen or broaden their minds creates a disturbing cycle of mental inactivity and decay. Certainly, the less people are challenged, the less they can perform. But research shows that older people can, and do, learn new things—and they learn them well. True, the limits of learning, and especially the pace of learning, are more restricted in age than in youth. And the conditions for successful learning are different for older people than for the young. The trouble is, our institutions of learning—schools and work organizations—have not yet adapted to these age differences. One result is that the myth about older people's capacity to grow and learn becomes further entrenched.

> *... current estimates are that no more than 10 percent of all elderly people, aged sixty-five to one hundred or more, are Alzheimer's patients.*

MacArthur research on mental function in old age is also encouraging. First of all, the fears of age-related loss are often exaggerated. Older people have become so sensitized to the threat of Alzheimer's disease that every forgotten name or misplaced key ring strikes fear. Alzheimer's is indeed a terrible disease, both for those afflicted and their caregivers. But current estimates are that no more than 10 percent of all elderly people, aged sixty-five to one hundred or more, are Alzheimer's patients. In fact, even among those aged seventy-four to eighty-one, a full half show no mental decline whatsoever over the following seven years. Ninety-five percent of older people live in the community at large; only 5 percent are in nursing homes. And that small percentage has been decreasing since 1982! The MacArthur Studies have added to our understanding of the factors that maintain high mental function. As we discuss in chapter 8, three key features predict strong mental function in old age: 1) regular physical activity; 2) a strong social support system; and 3) belief in one's ability to handle what life has to offer. Happily, all three can be initiated or increased, even in later life.

Older Men and Women Can and Do Learn New Things

Research has demonstrated the remarkable and enduring capacity of the aged brain to make new connections, absorb new data, and thus acquire new skills. In one experiment, older people who showed a decline in two important cognitive functions, inductive reasoning and spatial orientation, participated in five training sessions designed to improve these functions. The improvements were significant, and permanent. The same can be said of short-term memory among older men and women. Before training sessions, older people were able to recall fewer than five words from a randomly presented long list. After training, they were able to recall almost fifteen words. (In chapter 8, we go into this in more detail.) As consumers, older people learn to use household appliances that were unknown in their youth—food processors, microwave ovens, automated bank teller machines, and even "user-friendly" VCRs (video cassette recorders). Secretaries who learned their craft on manual typewriters make the transition to electric machines and then to word processors and computers.

The stereotype in organizations is that older people oppose innovation while younger ones urge it—the stereotypical old fogies versus the young Turks. But in fact, corporate battles often involve young fogies and old Turks! Intimate knowledge of a given organization, the security that often comes with long tenure and, ultimately, the freedom that accompanies impending retirement combine to yield significant advantages to older people in the workplace. Specifically, elders may have an innovative advantage that compensates for (or even exceeds) the flexibility of youth.

Some Aspects of Learning Are More Limited in Age

Science confirms what all of us have observed; young people tend to have sharper vision and better hearing than older people, their reaction time is quicker, and they outperform elders in terms of short-term memory. As a result, some kinds of learning, especially those that require perceptual speed, physical coordination, and muscular strength, become more difficult and ultimately impossible in old age. One of us (RLK) was, in his late teens, an aspiring gymnast. Robert mastered some modest feats, but the giant swing, in which the performer does a handstand on the high bar, was beyond his reach. Back then, he probably could have prevailed with a little extra training (and perhaps courage). At age eighty, the giant swing is beyond the realm of possibility. As we write this, however, we have before us a picture of the man who, as a senior Olympic competitor holds the national record for pole vault. He is sixty-seven years old! So while there are certainly limits, there are limit-breakers as well.

> *. . . elders may have an innovative advantage that compensates for (or even exceeds) the flexibility of youth.*

What It Takes to Learn Changes with Age

While it is true that older people have, in general, weaker short-term memories than younger people, these deficits can be overcome with proper training. For instance, older people can significantly improve their short-term memory by making lists and training their memory with practice games. Admittedly, similarly trained young people do still better, but trained elders often do better than trained young people.

There are many examples of ways in which older people can boost their performance when given the right opportunity for improvement. The key is for older people to develop at their own pace and with respect for both their practical and emotional needs. One good example is the case of a large company that was converting to computer-controlled operation of a decentralized staff. They soon found that older workers were relatively slow, and reluctant to adapt to the new procedures. Young people, already computer proficient, were assigned as coaches, but the difficulties continued. In time, older clerks were seen staying at their desks beyond the usual working hours, in order to practice in relative privacy and at their own pace. And indeed, their performance improved significantly. This episode illustrates several of the key requirements for learning new skills in old age. It is critical that older people be able to 1) work at their own pace; 2) practice new skills; and 3) avoid the embarrassment so common among older people when they cannot keep up to speed with their younger counterparts. From childhood, we become accustomed to older people teaching those who are younger. It is often difficult for older people to accept the reversal of roles in which the young become the mentors.

Teaching Institutions Haven't Adapted to Learning Needs

When it comes to learning, our society is still age-graded. Times have changed, the need for lifelong learning and relearning has increased, but our institutions have not caught up with the new realities. They operate as if life consisted of three compartmentalized periods—education, work, and retirement, in that order.

There was a time when that was adequate. The traditional skills of reading, writing, and arithmetic were sufficient for many jobs. More specific skills, once learned, were practiced for the rest of one's working life. That time is long gone. Technological change means that most people will need to learn several new jobs in the course of their working lives. We now know that the capacity to learn is lifelong. The next step will be to create the conditions under which lifelong learning can be nurtured and achieved.

MYTH # 3: "The Horse Is Out of the Barn"

We've all heard the claims of lifelong smokers that there's "no point stopping now"—the damage is already done and the habit permanently ingrained. This is an easy way out, but far from the truth. It's time to dispel the false and discouraging claim that old age is too late for efforts to reduce risk and promote health. Many older persons believe that after decades of risky behavior—overindulgence in alcohol and fat-laden food, lack of exercise, and so on—there is no point changing. They feel that what they have lost is gone forever and cannot be recovered, or they deny that their habits are dangerous in the first place. Many consider age-related change irreversible, and hold no hope for either recovering lost function or lessening their risks of developing diseases. Fortunately, they are mistaken. Not only can we recover much lost function and decrease risk, but in some cases we can actually increase function beyond our prior level.

Mark Twain amused his audiences by reversing the relationship between health and bad habits. He told a story about an elderly woman whose doctor, after careful examination, informed her that she would have to quit smoking, drinking, and gorging herself on rich food.

"But doctor," she protested, "I have never done any of those things in my life!"

At this point, Twain looked out at the audience. There was a moment of silence, he shook his white head sadly, and pronounced the grim verdict: "There you are. There was nothing to be done. She had neglected her habits!"

Certainly, it's better to start healthy habits early and sustain them for a lifetime. But for those who have strayed—that is, most people!—nature is remarkably forgiving. Research shows that it is almost never too late to begin healthy habits such as smoking cessation, sensible diet, exercise, and the like. And even more important, it is never too late to benefit from those changes. Making these changes can mark the transition from the risky state we call "usual aging" to the goal we all share: "successful aging"—growing old with good health, strength, and vitality.

Not only can we recover much lost function and decrease risk, but in some cases we can actually increase function beyond our prior level.

We're not, however, promoting a fantastical fountain of youth. Attempts at rejuvenation are probably as old as aging itself. Early in this century one of the more interesting (though ineffective) attempts involved injections of extracts of tiger testes. Though many anti-aging remedies and nostrums continue to be commercially available, most have little to offer or are, at best, of unproven value. We discuss these in greater detail in chapter 9. Despite the lack of proven "rejuvenators," however, there are many ways in which older people can recover function and decrease the risk of disease or disability. Perhaps the greatest anti-aging "potion" is good old-fashioned clean living.

Cigarette Smoking

Everyone knows that smoking is bad for the health. But we've heard it so often, and for so long, it often falls on deaf ears. Cigarette smoking and other tobacco use increases the risk of lung cancer and other lung diseases, coronary heart disease, stroke, and other life threatening illnesses. A person who smokes a pack of cigarettes a day is four times more likely than a nonsmoker to have coronary heart disease. Even a person who smokes less than half a pack a day is twice as likely to have coronary heart disease as a nonsmoker. That's the bad news.

The good news is that the risk of heart disease begins to fall almost as soon as you quit smoking—no matter how long you've smoked. Within a few months, smokers who have managed to quit begin to reap the benefits. In five years, an ex-smoker is not much more likely to have heart disease than a person who has never smoked! That's only part of the good news about smoking and heart disease. The rest of it is that the good effects of quitting smoking hold regardless of age, the number of years one smokes, or how heavy the smoking habit.

Like heart disease, the risk of stroke drops quickly when cigarette smoking stops. We know that among people aged thirty-four to fifty-five, those who stopped smoking within the past two to four years were no more at risk for stroke than those who had never smoked at all.

. . . the good effects of quitting smoking hold regardless of age, the number of years one smokes, or how heavy the smoking habit.

Lung disease, especially lung cancer and emphysema, is perhaps the main fear of cigarette smokers. In this case, too, the research is encouraging to former smokers and should spur those who are planning to stop. As with heart disease, the risk of lung cancer begins to fall when smoking stops, although much more slowly. It takes at least fifteen years after quitting for a smoker's risk of lung cancer to become as low as that of a lifetime non-smoker. But the good news remains; when you quit, your lungs begin to heal and the risk of lung disease begins to drop. That holds for people of all ages.

Being overweight and eating too much of the wrong things is like smoking in some ways. Psychologists call these activities oral gratification—and like smoking, eating habits are hard to change. Unfortunately, overeating is like smoking in another way: it increases the risk of many diseases. Several factors fit together like a puzzle and conspire to raise the risk of disease: eating too many calories, eating too much fat, and becoming obese. All of these—independently and as a group—may raise the risk of heart disease as well as certain cancers.

Syndrome X

Researchers have identified a new condition known as Syndrome X, in which a cluster of risk factors together raise the risk of heart attack and premature death. These factors include high blood sugar and insulin levels (the so-called pseudodiabetes of aging); high blood pressure; and increases in blood fats like cholesterol and triglycerides, which accompany the pot-bellied obesity so common in middle-aged and elderly people (especially men). But the good news for people with Syndrome X is that the increased risk of heart disease is related to their weight, not their age. When their weight drops and stays down, so do the risk factors for heart disease. These results hold in old age. When obese middle-aged and older men lose 10 percent of their body weight, they reduce their risk factors significantly. In one study, older men lost less weight than younger, but interestingly, they did almost as well in reducing their risk of disease.

High Blood Pressure

High blood pressure, especially the systolic blood pressure (the higher of the two numbers in your blood pressure reading), is an important risk factor for heart disease and stroke. In the United States and other similarly prosperous countries, systolic blood pressure generally rises with age. In fact, the increase in blood pressure is so common that it is often taken for granted, and considered the inevitable result of "normal" aging. But in developed countries, not *all* older people show increases in blood pressure; and on the flip side of the coin, in less-advantaged countries, where people eat less meat, more grains and vegetables, and keep physically active, blood pressure tends *not* to rise with age.

Diet and exercise tend to reduce blood pressure, but they are not failproof. Some people do neither, and have low blood pressure. And others do both, but are unable to lower their blood pressure to an acceptable level. In a reversal from previous practice, such older individuals are now commonly advised to take medication to get their blood pressure under control. But many older people resist drug treatment, arguing that they have tolerated their hypertension well for many years, and that certainly the damage is already done. But we now know that treatment of systolic hypertension is safe, inexpensive, and lowers risk. One large study, in which all the participants were over the age of sixty and some were over eighty, showed that drug treatments for high blood pressure reduced the risk of stroke by more than a third and the risk of heart attacks by more than a quarter. The horse may have been headed out of the barn, but some good rope tricks lured it back in.

Physical Witness

"Doc, I've been a couch potato for so many years, I can't possibly get back in shape" is a common refrain in my (JWR) office. Physical function does indeed decrease with age, especially in the realm of the upper limits of physical performance. The best race times of elderly marathon runners and master swimmers do not equal those of similarly trained young athletes (nor of their own performance in the days of their youth). Nerve function, heart capacity, kidney function, breathing capacity, and maximum work rate all show age-related reductions. Vision and hearing, muscle mass, and strength show similar age-related patterns. That's the bad news. But set against this tale of diminishing capacities are three reassuring facts.

First, the aged body is more than able to meet the demands of everyday life. Losses in elite athletic ability do not create handicaps for most activities.

Second, most age-related reductions in physical performance are avoidable and many are reversible. They are often the cumulative result of lifestyle—what we do with our bodies and what we take into them—rather than the result of aging itself. Years of cigarette smoking, excessive use of alcohol, too little exercise and too much food, especially fats and sugars, do physical damage that is often wrongly attributed to age.

The facts are that exercise dramatically increases physical fitness, muscle size, and strength in older individuals. Besides rejuvenating muscles, resistance exercises (pumping iron) also enhance bone

---

It turns out that active mental stimulation, and keeping up relationships with friends and relatives, also helps promote physical ability.

---

strength, limiting the risk of osteoporosis and fractures of the hip, spine, and wrist. Exercise also improves balance, thereby decreasing the risk of falling, a common and life-threatening problem in older persons. And as we discuss in detail in chapter 7, the MacArthur Studies now show that physical exercise is just the first of several ways to maintain one's physical abilities. It turns out that active mental stimulation, and keeping up relationships with friends and relatives, also helps promote physical ability. For instance, many people are surprised to learn that frequent emotional support (listening, encouragement, cheering up, understanding, and so on) is associated with improved physical function in old age. This is just one of countless connections between mind and body—mental vigor and physical well-being—that are seen in the aging process. A healthy physical and emotional lifestyle seems to be of even greater value to older people than younger ones. It's never too late to start.

MYTH # 4: "The Secret to Successful Aging Is to Choose Your Parents Wisely"

People commonly assume that genes (or heredity) account for the rate at which one's body functions decline with advancing age. And it's not hard to find examples to support that assumption—families in which everyone seems to live past ninety or not make it to age sixty-five. True, there is a meaningful connection between genetics and aging. For instance, it has long been recognized that the length of life of nonidentical twins varies much more than that of identical twins. But while the role of genetics in aging is important, it has been tremendously overstated. A common error is to assume that one's genetic predisposition is equivalent to genetic "control" of life expectancy, and that we are all preprogrammed for a given duration of life. Our MacArthur twin studies leave very substantial room for factors *other* than genetics in determining life expectancy.

When considering what factors promote long life, it is essential to distinguish familial habits and experiences from genes. Members of a family may share many characteristics as they grow old, but this should not be misinterpreted as evidence for a pure genetic role in aging. It is possible that these similarities are related more to common environmental conditions, such as diet, which are shared by family members. Not everything that runs in families is genetic. For example, apple pie recipes, though passed from generation to generation, are clearly not genetically determined. But the contents of those apple pies, and all other foods shared by families, have a meaningful impact on the health of all family members—their weight, blood sugar levels, you name it.

Regardless of our genes, we as individuals can play an important role in how successfully we age. Just how big a role can we play? That depends on the balance between the influence of genes and environment. Let's take a look at the ways in which heredity does—and does not—play an important role in the three key components of successful aging: 1) avoiding disease and disability; 2) maintaining high mental and physical function; and 3) continuing to engage actively in life, through productivity and strong interpersonal relationships.

The strongest influence of heredity on aging relates to genetic diseases that can shorten life, such as numerous forms of cancer and familial high cholesterol syndromes (which lead to heart disease). Certainly, it would behoove us to choose parents who don't carry genes for these diseases. Would that it were so easy. Still, however, heredity is not as powerful a player as many assume. For all but the most strongly determined genetic diseases, such as

Huntington's disease, MacArthur Studies show that the environment and lifestyle have a powerful impact on the likelihood of actually developing the disorder. This is wonderful news for individuals with strong family histories of some cancers, heart disease, hypertension, rheumatoid, arthritis, and many other conditions. We now know that diet, exercise, and even medications may delay, or completely eliminate, the emergence of the disease. Genes play a key role in promoting disease, but they are certainly less than half the story.

What about the role of genetics on mental and physical function, the second important component of successful aging? In this arena, MacArthur research has shown that heredity is *less* important than environment and lifestyle. A major study of Swedish twins that was part of the MacArthur Research Program on Successful Aging shed

---

For all but the most strongly determined genetic diseases, such as Huntington's disease, MacArthur Studies show that the environment and lifestyle have a powerful impact on the likelihood of actually developing the disorder.

---

light on the factors that influence the physiological changes that occur with advancing age. By studying both identical and nonidentical twins who were raised apart, researchers were able to tease apart the relative importance of heredity and environment on mental and physical changes with age. The bottom line is very clear: with rare exceptions, only about 30 percent of physical aging can be blamed on the genes. Additional studies of Swedish twins over the age of 80 show that only about half of the changes in mental function with aging are genetic. This leaves substantial room for a healthy lifestyle to protect the mind and body. And better yet, as we grow older, genetics becomes *less* important, and environment becomes *more* important. The likelihood of being fat, having hypertension, high cholesterol and triglyceride levels, and the rate at which one's lung function declines with advancing age are, by and large, largely *not* inherited. These risks are due to environmental or lifestyle factors. How we live, and where we live, has the most profound impact on age-related changes in the function of many organs throughout the body, including the heart, immune system, lung, bones, brain, and kidneys. We will discuss these important findings in greater detail in chapters 5-8.

The third component of successful aging, continuing active engagement with life, is for the most part not inherited. While certain personality traits may be, in part, heritable—the maintenance of good health certainly enhances the likelihood of remaining active and engaged in life—one's degree of vitality and interpersonal connection late in life is largely determined by *nongenetic* factors.

These findings are exceptionally optimistic and shatter the myth that our course in old age is predetermined. MacArthur research provides very strong scientific evidence that we are, in large part, responsible for our own old age. We have the powerful capacity to enhance our chance of maintaining high mental and physical ability as we grow older. Throughout this book, we will show you just how that can be accomplished.

MYTH # 5: "The Lights May Be on, but the Voltage Is Low"

This metaphorical assertion has at least three implications about aging—all negative and none accurate. The myth suggests that older people suffer from inadequate physical and mental abilities. And the electrical metaphor hints that older men and women are sexless, or at least uninterested in sex (and, in the case of men, unable to perform adequately regardless of interest). MacArthur research shows that while there is some modicum of truth to these beliefs, they're far more fiction than fact. Let's sift out the facts.

Sexuality in Old Age

At the time of this writing, a popular TV beverage commercial pokes fun at a silver-haired couple engaged in passionate foreplay on the living room couch. The image is presented as absurd, and a humorous reference is made to the parents (supposedly 100-plus years old) being home. Apparently, the age-old assumption that sexual interest and activity in later life are rare and inappropriate is still in full force. These stereotypical images are examples of what psychologists call "pluralistic ignorance"—that is, most people as private individuals know the image is false, but remain silent on the subject because they think that others see it as true.

We remind ourselves that myths do contain some truth. Sexual activity *does* tend to decrease in old age. However, there are tremendous individual differences in this intimate aspect of life. We know also that these differences are determined in part by cultural norms, by health or illness, and by the availability of sexual or romantic partners. When it comes to sexual activity, as in so many other aspects of aging, chronological age itself is not the critical factor. In men, the decline in testosterone with age is highly variable and linked only loosely with sexual performance.

Certainly there are older people who have lost interest in sex and are glad to be done with it. When Sophocles, the great tragic poet of ancient Greece, was in his eighties, he was asked rather delicately whether, at his advanced age, he "had yet any acquaintance with Venus." "Heavens forbid!" the sage is said to have replied, "I thank the gods that I am finally rid of that tyranny."

Had surveys been conducted in the Greece of 400 B.C., it is unlikely that all of his elderly countrymen (and women) would have agreed with him. Certainly it is not the dominant view of older men and women in the United States today. There is a gradual decline in sexual interest and ability beginning around the age of fifty. How-

> *When it comes to sexual activity, as in so many other aspects of aging, chronological age itself is not the critical factor.*

ever, this decline has many causes besides age itself, including certain chronic diseases and the medications with which they are treated. Diabetes, heart disease, and hypertension are perhaps the most frequent impediments to sexual function, especially for men.

At least since the famous Kinsey report in 1953, there have been occasional attempts to put numbers to the question of sexual activity in old age. One important early study found that at age sixty-eight, about 70 percent of men were sexually active on a regular basis. At age seventy-eight, however, the percentage dropped to about 25 percent of men. In addition to age itself, health status was the major factor in determining the frequency of sexual activity among men. For older women, however, regularity of sexual activity depends primarily on the availability of an appropriate partner. If this study were repeated today, the substantial improvements in health among older people and the changes in social norms that have occurred during the past two decades would likely yield evidence of even greater interest and participation in sex in later life.

Finally, our wish list for research on this important subject includes a distinction between the sex act itself and the many other norms of physical intimacy. The basic human need for affectionate physical contact, which is apparent even in newborn infants, persists throughout life. The voltage is never too low for that—in fact, it may help keep the lights on.

MYTH # 6: "The Elderly Don't Pull Their Own Weight"

The widespread belief that older people are relatively unproductive in society is wrong and unjust in three ways: 1) the measures of performance are wrong; our society doesn't count a great deal of productive activity; 2) the playing field is not level; older men and women aren't given an equal chance for paying jobs; and 3) millions of older people are ready, willing, and able to increase their productivity, paid and voluntary. Let's look at the facts that bear on each of these claims.

The Measures Are Wrong

The accusation that older people are burdens rather than contributors to society is heard in many places, from the halls of Congress to the living rooms of overworked young men and women. The unstated assumptions are that everybody who works for pay is pulling his or her weight, and that everyone who does not work for pay is a burden.

Both assumptions are wrong. Some people who are paid do little or nothing useful, and some are paid to do things that are damaging—writing advertisements for cigarettes, for example. It is ironic and misleading, as well as unfair, that such things are counted as productive, while raising children, maintaining a household, taking care of an ill or disabled family member, or working as a volunteer in a hospital or church are considered unproductive (or at least not "counted" as productive). While it is important to distinguish between paid and unpaid work, it is wrong to omit unpaid productive work from our national accounting. As people age, and especially as they retire from paid work, their continuing productive activities are increasingly unpaid. Our national statistics thus ignore a great deal of productive activity, a great deal of what keeps our society functioning.

Almost all older men and women are productive in this larger sense. One-third work for pay and one-third work as volunteers in churches, hospitals, and other organizations. Others provide informal, much-needed assistance to family members, friends, and neighbors. It would take more than three million paid caregivers, working full time, to provide that assistance to sick and disabled people!

In 1997, a national campaign was mounted to increase volunteerism in America. The president and several ex-presidents spoke of the country's need for voluntary activity and urged people to contribute as volunteers. We propose one way of making it more attractive to volunteer: start counting voluntary work as productive. The ways we measure productive activity are broken; fix them!

The Playing Field Is Not Level

Older men and women aren't given an equal chance for paid employment. Retirement used to be compulsory. When you reached the ages of fifty-five or sixty or sixty-five, you had to retire. While it is now illegal to force people to retire solely because of their age, downsizing, corporate mergers, and other organizational changes affect older people disproportionately. For many people retirement, while not legally compelled, is nevertheless involuntary.

In addition to the stick of involuntary retirement, there is the carrot of pension entitlements, both private and through Social Security. These make retirement attractive or, for some, downright irresistible. We should remember, however, that the reasons for creating Social Security in the first place were not only to prevent poverty in old age but also to make way for youth. In an economy plagued by unemployment, getting older workers out of the labor force was an attractive idea. It exchanged unwanted joblessness among younger people for a more acceptable kind of joblessness (retirement) at the other end of the age range. In combination, both public and private policies urge older people to retire and we then blame them for doing so.

In combination, both public and private policies urge older people to retire and we then blame them for doing so.

Older people who want to continue working beyond the usual retirement age see the inflexibility of employers as the main obstacle. Many of those who are still working and would like to continue with the same employer want fewer hours, a change in work content, or greater flexibility in scheduling. Ninety percent of those who want such changes, however, say that their employers will not accommodate them. Older people who are seeking new jobs report that companies are reluctant to hire older workers. Many employers seem to believe, mistakenly, that older workers are less productive, more often absent, or are liabilities in some other respect. When it comes to job-hunting by older people, the playing field has yet to be leveled.

They Are Ready, Willing, and Able

When Old Age and Survivors Insurance (OASI) was first enacted, most people did not live to the legal retirement age of sixty-five years. Most of those who did, it was assumed, would be neither willing nor able to work. Since the early twentieth century, life expectancy has greatly increased and the health of older people has greatly improved. Although some are not able to work and some do not wish to work, there are millions of older men and women who are ready, willing, and able to work. Among nonworkers aged fifty to fifty-nine, almost half would prefer to work, and among those sixty to sixty-four, more than one-third agree. Companies that have emphasized the recruitment and retention of older workers confirm that older employees meet or surpass expectations, often bringing the added value of increased insight and experience to the work environment.

Another Country *and* Xenophobia: Our Fears Divide Us[3]

BY MARY PIPHER, PH.D.
EXCERPTS FROM THE BOOK *ANOTHER COUNTRY: NAVIGATING THE EMOTIONAL TERRAIN OF OUR ELDERS*

Chapter 1: Another Country

> The trouble is, old age is not interesting until one gets there. It's a foreign country with an unknown language to the young and even to the middle-aged.

> —MAY SARTON,
> *As We Are Now*

The metaphor of aging and death as visiting another country is at least 1,500 years old. Thomas Cahill quotes St. Patrick in his book *How the Irish Saved Civilization:* "In the end, your hungers are rewarded: you are going home. Look, your ship is ready." Old age, especially in the last hard years, is really a search for a place in the universe, both figuratively and literally. The old look for their existential place. They ask, "How did my life matter?" "Was my time well spent?" "What did I mean to others?" "What can I look back on with pride?" "Did I love the right people?" And they search for a home and a village where they will be comfortable, useful, and loved.

This search for place becomes the central issue during people's final years. Family members want to help, but we live in a culture in which this journey into another country is hard for everyone. We are scattered across the continent living hurried, scheduled lives. We have few road maps to help us navigate the new lands. Aging in America is harder than it needs to be.

As we approach the millennium, we are entering a new territory, with very different family structures, work options, kinds of old age, and choices about living situations and health care. Earlier in the century, Robert Frost wrote, "Home is the place where, when you have to go there, they have to take you in." That has been less true in the last half of our century.

---

3. Excerpted from *Another Country* by Mary Pipher, Ph.D. Copyright ©1999 by Mary Pipher, Ph.D. Reprinted with permission.

Families are struggling with all the common problems of aging relatives plus the new dilemmas of the nineties. There aren't many rituals to guide us. Asian, Native American, and African-American cultures have rich traditions of caring for the aged, but nobody is prepared for managed care or housing units that require $200,000 deposits. In short, we are not ready for today.

We've experienced enormous demographic changes across this century. In 1900, the life expectancy at birth was forty-nine; today it is seventy-six. Today one family in four is caring for an older relative. As James Atlas wrote in "The Sandwich Generation" in *The New Yorker*, soon, for the first time in history, many middle-aged people will have more parents alive than they have children. He bemoaned the distance between modern parents and children: "Geographic freedom means we are dispersed." He wrote of the hassles of caring for children and parents at the same time: "All of a sudden you must rescue the people you thought were superhuman. To see your parents as vulnerable is hard. At the same time you feel sorry for yourself. It's tough on your own kids. You want to spend time with them but there are only so many hours in the day."

> *We don't have the resources, the rituals, or the institutions to make our old feel like elders.*

We are in a new world with no real prototypes for dealing with all these aging people. Medicine has both helped and complicated our situation. Many people live longer and healthier lives. But unhealthy people live longer, too. We have thousands of citizens who lie comatose in long-term health-care facilities. Bodies last longer than brains, support systems, or savings accounts. We don't have the resources, the rituals, or the institutions to make our old feel like elders.

There is an urgency to understand and accommodate an aging culture because most of us baby boomers have aged relatives. We are the pig in the python, the big demographic bulge that has moved across the last half of our century. What happens to us happens to millions of people at once. Right now our parents are becoming old people.

Of course, everything we do to help the old surely will help us all later on. Soon our country will be avalanched by old people, and those people will be us. In a few decades, our solutions to the dilemmas of caring for our elders will be applied to our own lives. The kindness, the indifference, the ignorance, and the wisdom will be passed on. The more we love and respect our elders, the more we teach our children to love and respect us. The more we think through problems today, the more organizational and cultural structures will be in the place to handle our generation's needs.

Right now we don't even know how to talk about our problems. We have no language for nurturing interdependency. The traditional ways of caring for our parents don't work, and new ways haven't been invented. Decisions about living arrangements, money, and health are complicated, and much of the information that would help is not available. We don't really know how long we or our parents will be healthy, what will happen to the economy, or how much medical care will cost.

Our general confusion is compounded by a new kind of ignorance. Until late in this century, we humans spent time with people of all generations, but today we aren't likely to have much contact with old people until we are relatively old ourselves. We baby boomers live in what Robert Bly calls "sibling societies," and we are educated away from relationships with our elders. We are not taught how interesting they are. We don't know their needs, and they don't know ours.

> *Until late in this century, we humans spent time with people of all generations, but today we aren't likely to have much contact with old people until we are relatively old ourselves.*

Many old people live in segregated communities. Some choose to live separately from the young—they don't like their noise and bother—but most just slowly become more isolated. For example, I know an Italian immigrant who moved into an assisted-living unit for health reasons. He deeply misses his old neighborhood, his friends of a lifetime, his grandchildren, the cafe on the corner that served real Italian pizza, and his boccie-ball-playing buddies.

We group people by age. We put our three-year-olds together, our thirteen-year-olds together, and our eighty-year-olds together. Children and teenagers can go months at a time with no contact with the old. Adolescent peer culture is especially noxious, but so are the cultures of isolated day-care centers or senior citizens' homes.

A great deal of the social sickness in America comes from this age segregation. If ten fourteen-year-olds are grouped together, they will fight with one another. They will form a "lord of the flies" culture with its competitiveness, social anxiety, and meanness. But if ten people aged two to eighty are grouped together, they will fall into a natural age hierarchy that nurtures and teaches all of them. Because each person has a niche, competition will subside. Each person will have something unique to contribute. Values will deepen, and experience will grow richer. For our own mental and societal health, we need to reconnect the age groups.

My client Irena just returned from visiting her parents in a Southwestern retirement community. She talked about how depressing it was, rows of identical suburban houses baking in the 110-degree weather. There was no one on the streets. Pollution and heat kept everyone trapped in air-conditioned houses, "waiting to die," as Irena put it. "My parents' lives have become their medical conditions," she told me. "It was the worst week of my life."

The two biggest changes over the course of this century have been our move from a pre-psychology to a post-psychology culture and our move from a communal to an individualistic culture. Most older people grew up surrounded by family. They shared bedrooms with half a dozen siblings and had grandparents or great-aunts in their homes or living nearby. They knew their neighbors, and their fun was other people. They tend to be gregarious and communal and turn towards others for support and entertainment.

The two biggest changes over the course of this century have been our move from a pre-psychology to a post-psychgology culture and our move from a communal to an individualistic culture.

There are very real cultural differences between generations that create what I call time-zone problems. Generations have different attitudes about everything from authority to expressing feelings to R-rated movies. The generations have different attitudes even toward attitudes. My generation is more comfortable being sacrilegious, skeptical, and ironic.

Our parents' generation was pre-irony. Of course, some people were ironic, but most were not. Irony implies a distance between one's words and one's world, a cool remove that is a late-century phenomenon. One theory is that irony became widespread in this country during World War I, when soldiers realized the gap between their own experiences and civilian perceptions. Freud also helped create the culture of irony. He gave my generation the notion that underneath one idea is another, that behind our surface behavior is a different motive. Advertising also layers meaning in a way that teaches ironic thinking. There is an apparent message, and a subliminal message about something very different. By now we all learn to think ironically. But many people older than a certain age grew up believing that the surface is all there is.

The old, like the young, come in all varieties. However, differences aside, there are some things we can say about the old as a group. The old are segregated by interests, by history, by physical health, by attitudes about mental health, and by shared trauma. They have in common three sets of experiences—they have participated in the events of the twentieth century, they have passed through the same developmental hurdles, and they now live in the landscape of old age.

They have lived before television, cars, electricity, *Playboy*, and the Green Revolution. Older African-Americans had parents who remembered slavery. Older Native Americans had relatives who fought in the Indian wars of the last century. Rural old men know how to mend harnesses, butcher hogs, build fences, cut hay, slice the testicles off a bull, and fix an engine. Older women can bake, quilt, make soap, sew trousers, and doctor sick animals. Many of the old know how to play instruments, sketch portraits, and recite poetry.

Older people have passed through seven of Erik Erikson's eight stages of development. Middle age is in the distant past. Most of the old have been parents and grandparents. They have lost parents, siblings, and friends. They have seen vigorous bodies grow frail, and active minds grow forgetful.

In his book *The Summing Up,* Somerset Maugham noted that with old age, one is free of certain passions. Most people become less sexual, less competitive, and less envious. Most people have figured out that life is tough for everyone. They tend to be kinder and more compassionate than they were as young people. . . . Generally, the old like verbal and physical affection and, unlike the young, are under no illusion that they do not need love. . . .

Chapter 2: Xenophobia: Our Fears Divide Us

Few of them made it to thirty.
Old age was the privilege of rocks and trees.
Childhood ended as fast as wolf cubs grow.
One had to hurry, to get on with life
before the sun went down,
before the first snow.

—Wislawa Szymborska,
"Our Ancestors' Short Lives"

We segregate the old for many reasons—prejudice, ignorance, a lack of good alternatives, and a youth-worshiping culture without guidelines on how to care for the old. The old are different from us, and that makes us nervous. Xenophobia means fear of people from another country. In America we are xenophobic toward our old people.

An anthropologist could learn about us by examining our greeting cards. As with all aspects of popular culture, greeting cards both mirror and shape our realities. Cards reflect what we feel about people in different roles, and they also teach us what to feel. I visited my favorite local drugstore and took a look.

There are really two sets of cards that relate to aging. One is the grandparent/grandchild set that is all about connection. Even a very dim-witted anthropologist would sense the love and respect that exist between these two generations in our culture. Young children's cards to their grandparents say, "I wish I could hop on your lap," or, "You're so much fun." Grandparents' cards to children are filled with pride and love.

There is another section of cards on birthdays. These compare human aging to wine aging, or point out compensations. "With age comes wisdom, of course that doesn't make up for what you lose." We joke the most about that which makes us anxious. "Have you picked out your bench at the mall yet?" There are jokes about hearing loss, incontinence, and losing sexual abilities and interest. There are cards on saggy behinds, gray hair, and wrinkles, and cards about preferring chocolate or sleep to sex. "You know you're getting old when someone asks if you're getting enough and you think about sleep."

Poking fun at aging isn't all bad. . . However, these jokes reflect our fears about aging in a youth-oriented culture.

Poking fun at aging isn't all bad. It's better to laugh than to cry, especially at what cannot be prevented. However, these jokes reflect our fears about aging in a youth-oriented culture. We younger, healthier people sometimes avoid the old to avoid our own fears of aging. If we aren't around dying people, we don't have to think about dying.

We baby boomers have been a futureless generation, raised in the eternal present of TV and advertising. We have allowed ourselves to be persuaded by ads that teach that if we take good care of ourselves to be persuaded by ads that teach that if we take good care of ourselves, we will stay healthy. Sick people, hospitals, and funerals destroy our illusions of invulnerability. They force us to think of the future.

Carolyn Heilbrun said, "It is only past the meridian of fifty that one can believe that the universal sentence of death applies to oneself." Before that time, if we are healthy, we are likely to be in deep denial about death, to feel as if we have plenty of time, that we have an endless vista ahead. But in hospitals and at funerals, we remember that we all die in the last act. And we don't necessarily appreciate being reminded.

When I first visited rest homes, I had to force myself to stay. What made me most upset was the thought of myself in a place like that. I didn't want to go there, literally or figuratively. Recently I sat in an eye doctor's office surrounded by old people with white canes. Being in this room gave me intimations of mortality. I thought of Bob Dylan's line: "It's not dark yet, but it's getting there."

We know the old-old will die soon. The more we care and the more involved we are with the old, the more pain we feel at their suffering. Death is easier to bear in the abstract, far away and clinical. It's much harder to watch someone we love fade before our eyes. It's hard to visit an uncle in a rest home and realize he no longer knows who we are or even who he is. It's hard to see a grandmother in pain or drugged up on morphine. Sometimes it's so hard that we stay away from the people who need us the most.

> *Our culture reinforces our individual fears. To call something old is to insult, as in old hat or old ideas.*

Our culture reinforces our individual fears. To call something old is to insult, as in *old hat* or *old ideas*. To call something young is to compliment, as in *young thinking* or *young acting*. It's considered rude even to ask an old person's age. When we meet an adult we haven't seen in a long time, we compliment her by saying, "You haven't aged at all." The taboos against acknowledging age tell us that aging is shameful.

Many of the people I interviewed were uncomfortable talking about age and were unhappy to be labeled old. They said, "I don't feel old." What they meant was, "I don't act and feel like the person who the stereotypes suggest I am." Also, they were trying to avoid being put in a socially undesirable class. In this country, it is unpleasant to be called old, just as it is unpleasant to be called fat or poor. The old naturally try to avoid being identified with an unappreciated group.

In *The Coming of Age*, Simone de Beauvoir wrote about France in the 1600s, when the average life span was twenty to twenty-five. Exhausting labor, bad hygiene, and undernourishment led to early deaths. Those who did survive longer often gave their homes to their children. Similarly, in Ireland the old were moved into a room called the "western chamber," and the adult children took over the house.

De Beauvoir found a wide range of cultural responses to grandparents. In some subsistence cultures with harsh climates, the old were often left behind or out to die. In Greenland, the aged Amassalik killed themselves so they wouldn't be a burden. When they could no longer keep up, the old Hmong people were left with food and opium along mountain trails. But in most cultures, the feelings between children and grandparents were of great love and tenderness. Elders were considered serene, detached, and holy.

In some primitive societies, old people were valued as a source of stored knowledge. The Aleuts had great respect for their elders, who taught them to fish. The Navahos revered the old singers, who remembered all the tribal stories. The Kikuyu had sayings such as "An old person doesn't spit without a reason," and "Old people don't tell lies." De Beauvoir also found a strong relationship between the compassionate treatment of the old and the caring treatment of the young. Children who grew up well-nurtured tended to love the old.

The Okinawans have great respect for their elders. The old stay in their own homes, socialize with friends and family, and keep working a few hours a day. A ninety-year-old woman still sells fish. Friends will buy a little from her so that she has a useful routine. An eighty-year-old house-keeper will stop over to make sweet potato pancakes and sweep the steps. Many people live to be more than a hundred and stay in remarkably good health. The average age of death for women is eighty-four. Among people who stay on the island, there is little cancer, diabetes, osteoporosis, or stroke, but if Okinawans move away, they have the same mortality rates as others.

> *In some primitive societies, old people were valued as a source of stored knowledge.*

Joe Starita, author of *The Dull Knifes of Pine Ridge*, talked about the differences between the way most Americans view the elderly and the way the Lakota view their elders. "For starters," he said, "there is a tremendous difference in the words elderly and elder." The Lakota believe that if the old do not stay connected to the young, the culture will disintegrate. Older people tell stories that teach lessons and keep the culture alive. Because wisdom is highly valued among the Lakota, the older people are, the more they are loved. Older equals wiser equals more respected.

One Sunday afternoon Starita visited Royal Bull Bear on the Pine Ridge reservation. They were sitting at his kitchen table drinking coffee when two pickups pulled into his drive. His three daughters jumped out of one truck with bags of groceries. They greeted their father casually and then got to work. Two of them cleaned his house from top to bottom. They changed his bed linens, swept, and washed floors and windows. The other made him a pot of soup and sandwiches for the next week. Meanwhile the boys from the other pickup mowed his yard, picked up his trash, and changed the oil in his truck. Then they all hugged and kissed him good-bye and drove off. Royal Bull Bear said that this happens every Sunday. It is their duty to care for him.

Starita marveled that in such a "poor" society there is so much generosity of time and money toward the elders. There is a richness of caring among the Lakota that he found missing in most of America. I thought of Mother Teresa's remarks about America being one of the poorest cultures in the world. She had noticed a spiritual poverty here, a lack of connection and meaning. . . .

When we think of the old, most of us picture our grandparents. I see my grandmother in her flowered apron, and my grandfather in overalls and a felt hat. But old people today don't much resemble the grandparents of the 1950s. The young-old travel, program computers, study at Elderhostels, and take scuba lessons, or at least

> *Because of economic and demographic changes, as well as technological changes in health care, the old-old have existential decisions to make that our grandparents never had to face.*

they do until they join the ranks of the old-old. Because of economic and demographic changes, as well as technological changes in health care, the old-old have existential decisions to make that our grandparents never had to face.

We know less about the aged than we think we do. There is a lack of good information about the developmental, psychological, social, and spiritual needs of the old. We can empathize with children because we have been young. We remember some of what happened and how it felt. However, we haven't had experiences that allow us to understand the old.

In general there is a tendency to pretend the old are more like us than they really are. We underestimate the differences between adults and children, and we ignore differences in the characters and points of view of our elders. The old-old especially face very different physical, social, and psychological problems than do the rest of us.

Most of us love particular old people, and we want to do the right things for them. But we often don't understand what the right things are. For example, we are encouraged to buy things for the old, but what most older people want is our time. Gifts of attention are much prized. One of my neighbors recently had her eightieth birthday, and I wondered what to buy her. She lives in a small apartment and already has too much stuff. She can't see to read and can't eat candy or most food treats. Finally I decided simply to buy her a few flowers and deliver them. She liked the flowers, but afterward I realized what she liked most was the chance to show me her apartment and have a cup of tea.

My friend Karen travels across our state every Mother's Day to plant a garden for her mother. Louis's mother had a tracheotomy and can no longer talk. He taught her to use e-mail to stay connected to family. Chris attends a university a few blocks from his grandmother's home. He lives with her and does her errands and yard work. She fixes him meals and helps him with his German, which is her native language.

The old also want our honesty. When my client Carmen got a divorce, she tried to protect her grandmother from the news. Grannie was ill in a rest home and, in Carmen's opinion, she didn't need any bad news. Week after week, Carmen chatted away about cooking and window treatments while Grannie watched her closely and said little. Carmen thought she was being kind, but Grannie felt excluded, confused, and frightened. After six weeks, Grannie blurted out her questions: "What's wrong? You're losing weight, and your fingernails are chewed to the bone. Have you stopped trusting me? Do I have cancer? Do you have cancer? Did your husband die?" Carmen realized that she'd been protecting Grannie from honesty, a chance to help, and a genuine relationship—things all sane people want to experience.

Because food and love are so closely associated for our parents' generation, gifts of food can be powerful. Stopping by with a pecan pie or a pot of homemade soup is appreciated as an act of love. People who are in institutions or hospitals particularly welcome the tastes and smells of the real world. Once when my mother-in-law had been hospitalized for several days, I stopped at a Chinese restaurant and bought her a carton of hot and sour soup. I carried it to her hospital room, and that spicy aroma from the outside world revived her. Her spirits and her health improved.

Nothing in our culture guides us in a positive way toward the old. Our media, music, and advertising industries all glorify the young. Stereotypes suggest that older people keep younger people from fun, work, and excitement. They take time (valuable time) and patience (in very short supply in the 1990s). We are very body-oriented, and old bodies fail. We are appearance-oriented, and youthful attractiveness fades. We are not taught that old spirits often shimmer with beauty.

Language is a problem. Old people are referred to in pejorative terms, such as *biddy, codger,* or *geezer,* or with cutesy words, such as *oldster, chronologically challenged,* or *senior citizen.* People describe themselves as "eighty years young." Even *retirement* is an ugly word that implies passivity, uselessness, and withdrawal from the social and working world. Many of the old are offended by ageist stereotypes and jokes. Some internalize these beliefs and feel badly about themselves. They stay with their own kind in order to avoid the harsh appraisals of the young.

Some people do not have good manners with the old. I've seen the elderly bossed around, treated like children or simpletons, and simply ignored. Once in a cafe, I heard a woman order her mother to take a pill and saw the mother wince in embarrassment. My mother-in-law says she sees young people but they don't see her. Her age makes her invisible.

In our culture the old are held to an odd standard. They are admired for not being a bother, for being chronically cheerful. They are expected to be interested in others, bland in their opinions, optimistic, and emotionally generous. But the young certainly don't hold themselves to these standards.

> *Many of the old are offended by ageist stereotypes and jokes. Some internalize these beliefs and feel badly about themselves.*

Accidents that old drivers have are blamed on age. After a ninety-year-old friend had his first car accident, he was terrified that he would lose his license. "If I were young, this accident would be perceived as just one of those things," he pointed out. "But because I am old, it will be attributed to my age." Now, of course, some old people are bad drivers. But so are some young people. To say "He did that because he's old" is often as narrow as to say, "He did that because he's black" or "Japanese." Young people burn countertops with hot pans, forget appointments, and write overdrafts on their checking accounts. But when the old do these same things, they experience double jeopardy. Their mistakes are not viewed as accidents but rather as loss of functioning. Such mistakes have implications for their freedom.

As in so many other areas, the media hurts rather than helps with our social misunderstandings. George Gerbner reported on the curious absence of media images of people older than sixty-five. Every once in a while a romantic movie plot might involve an older man, but almost never an older woman. In general, the old have been cast as silly, stubborn, and eccentric. He also found that on children's programs, older women bear a disproportionate burden of negative characteristics. In our culture, the old get lumped together into a few stereotyped images: the sweet old lady, the lecherous old man, or the irascible but soft-hearted grandfather. Almost no ads and billboards feature the old. Every now and then an ad will show a grandparent figure, but then the grandparent is invariably youthful and healthy.

In *Fountain of Age,* Betty Friedan noted that the old are portrayed as sexless, demented, incontinent, toothless, and childish. Old women are portrayed as sentimental, naive, and silly gossips, and as troublemakers. A common movie plot is the portrayal of the old trying to be young—showing them on motorbikes, talking hip or dirty, or liking rock and roll. Of course there are exceptions, such as *Nobody's Fool, On Golden Pond, Mr. and Mrs. Bridge, Driving Miss Daisy, Mrs. Brown,* and *Twilight.* But we need more movies in which old people are portrayed in all their diversity and complexity.

The media is only part of much larger cultural problems. We aren't organized to accommodate this developmental stage. For example, being old-old costs a lot of money. Assisted-living housing, medical care, and all the other services the old need are expensive. And yet, most old people can't earn money. It's true that some of our elders are wealthy, but many live on small incomes. Visiting the old, I heard tragic stories involving money. I met Arlene, who, while dying of cancer, had to fear losing her house because of high property taxes. I met Shirley, who lived on noodles and white rice so that she could buy food for her cat and small gifts for her grandchildren. I met people who had to choose between pills and food or heat.

Almost no ads and billboards feature the old. Every now and then an ad will show a grandparent figure, but then the grandparent is invariably youthful and healthy.

Another thing that makes old age a difficult stage to navigate is our American belief that adults need no one. We think of independence as the ideal state for adults. We associate independence with heroes and cultural icons such as the Marlboro man and the Virginia Slims woman, and we associate dependence with toxic families, enmeshment, and weakness. To our postmodern, educated ears, a psychologically healthy but dependent adult sounds oxymoronic.

We all learn when we are very young to make our own personal declarations of independence. In our culture, *adult* means "self-sufficent." Autonomy is our highest virtue. We want relationships that have no strings attached instead of understanding, as one lady told me, "Honey, life ain't nothing but strings."

These American ideas about independence hurt families with teens. Just when children most need guidance from parents, they turn away from them and toward peers and media. They are socialized to believe that to be an adult, they must break away from parents. Our ideas about independence also hurt families with aging relatives. As people move from the young-old stage into the old-old stage, they need more help. Yet in our culture we provide almost no graceful ways for adults to ask for help. We make it almost impossible to be dependent yet dignified, respected, and in control.

As people age, they may need help with everything from their finances to their driving. They may need help getting out of bed, feeding themselves, and bathing. Many would rather pay strangers, do without help, or even die than be dependent on those they love. They don't want to be a burden, the greatest of American crimes. The old-old often feel ashamed of what is a natural stage of the life cycle. In fact, the greatest challenge for many elders is learning to accept vulnerability and to ask for help.

If we view life as a time line, we realize that all of us are sometimes more and sometimes less dependent on others. At certain stages we are caretakers, and at other stages we are cared for. Neither stage is superior to the other. Neither implies pathology or weakness. Both are just the results of life having seasons and circumstances. In fact, good mental health is not a matter of being dependent or independent, but of being able to accept the stage one is in with grace and dignity. It's an awareness of being, over the course of one's lifetime, continually interdependent.

> *... in our culture we provide almost no graceful ways for adults to ask for help. We make it almost impossible to be dependent yet dignified, respected, and in control.*

In our culture the old fear their deaths will go badly, slowly, and painfully, and will cost lots of money. Nobody wants to die alone, yet nobody wants to put their families through too much stress. Families are uneasy as they negotiate this rocky terrain. The trick for the younger members is to help without feeling trapped and overwhelmed. The trick for older members is to accept help while preserving dignity and control. Caregivers can say, "You have nurtured us, why wouldn't we want to nurture you?" The old must learn to say, "I am grateful for your help and I am still a person worthy of respect."

As our times and circumstances change, we need new language. We need the elderly to become elders. We need a word for the neediness of the old-old, a word with less negative connotations than *dependency,* a word that connotes wisdom, connection, and dignity. *Dependency* could become *mutuality* or *interdependency.* We can say to the old: "You need us now, but we needed you and we will need our children. We need each other."

However, the issues are much larger than simply which words to use or social skills to employ. We need to completely rethink our ideas about caring for the elderly. Like the Lakota, we need to see it as an honor and an opportunity to learn. It is our chance to repay our parents for the love they gave us, and it is our last chance to become grown-ups. We help them to help ourselves.

We need to make the old understand that they can be helped without being infantilized, that the help comes from respect and gratitude rather than from pity or a sense of obligation. In our society of disposables and planned obsolescence, the old are phased out. Usually they fade away graciously. They want to be kind and strong, and, in America, they learn that to do so means they should ask little of others and not bother young people .

Perhaps we need to help them redefine kindness and courage. For the old, to be kind ought to mean welcoming younger relatives' help, and to be brave ought to mean accepting the dependency that old-old age will bring. We can reassure the old that by showing their children how to cope, they will teach them and their children how well this last stage can be managed. This information is not peripheral but rather something everyone will need to know. . . .

V. A Time of New Possibilities

Editor's Introduction

Researching the topic of aging in America, one is likely to encounter many references to "productive" or "positive" aging, an alluring concept that is the subject of this book's final section. There are undoubtedly many different and equally valid interpretations of what this notion entails. What types of pursuits and what kinds of attitudes help make life's later years as fulfilling as possible? The answers here, in the form of the following articles, struck me as unusual and unexpected. Since I could include only a few, they do not begin to represent the myriad pursuits of older people. Furthermore, they are in no way meant to prescribe how one *should* spend one's later years; rather they are merely a few possibilities that may challenge some of the conventional stereotypes and expand readers' notions of what this time in life can be about.

Elderhostel was founded in 1975, based on the principle that "learning is a lifelong process that is rewarding at every age." By the mid-1990s, more than 300,000 people over age 55 participated annually in Elderhostel programs, which were being hosted by 1,800 organizations such as universities, field stations, and cultural and environmental centers worldwide. In Sara Rimer's "An Alaska Trek Makes Elders of the Aging" (*New York Times),* she relates one Elderhostel trip. The participants embark on an adventure in which they sleep in makeshift cabins, catch and clean fish for their dinners, and trek across Arctic tundra. They are also exposed to a cultural perception of aging that differs markedly from the prevailing Western norm, one in which the aged are regarded not as senior citizens but as "elders."

While Elderhostel trips are comparatively affordable, not all older people enjoy the good health or financial wherewithal to travel. Time, however, is a resource available to the majority of them, and many use it to pursue activities that may have been unthinkable during earlier, busier years. In another article by Sara Rimer, "Turning to Autobiography for Emotional Growth in Old Age" (*New York Times*), she reports on members of a writing group who range in age from their mid-60s to their mid-80s. The group, Rimer says, is one of thousands across the country whose members gather to share their life stories. "It's made me admit I've had a hell of a life," said Bob Harvey, a workshop participant in Galveston, Texas. "I never thought about it before."

In his recent book, *The Virtues of Aging,* former U.S. president Jimmy Carter reflects on his own journey toward old age. Although many would consider Mr. Carter an exceptionally fortunate and successful man, the latter period of his life has not always been easy. He begins his book by recounting the deep disappointment he felt upon being forced into "early retirement" after losing the 1980 presidential election to Ronald Regan, then describes how, when he returned to private life, he found himself hugely in debt and in danger of losing his family farm. He recovered from these difficulties and, after initial apprehension, now considers his later years to be the best of his life. While the other articles in this section describe specific activities in which older people engage, in the excerpt included here, Mr. Carter articulates an ideology. He outlines his own vision of "successful aging," describing what he feels should be the focus of our later years: namely, personal happiness, a willingness to take risks, and our relationships with others. If, Mr. Carter believes, we nurture these goals, our later years, like his own, may be the most rewarding.

An Alaska Trek Makes Elders of the Aging[1]

BY SARA RIMER
NEW YORK TIMES, SEPTEMBER 2, 1998

Martha Wroe made up her mind years ago that there were two things she would never do when she got old. "I was not going to be one of those old ladies clutching their purses to them wherever they went," she said. Nor was she going to be the sort of traveler who viewed the world from the safety of a cruise ship.

Which was why, three weeks shy of her 77th birthday, Ms. Wroe was bracing herself against the wind as she made her way across a stretch of rain-soaked tundra on Alaska's northwest coast, 26 miles above the Arctic Circle, wearing a fanny pack. This old lady had left her purse behind, in Gainesville, Fla.

"I wanted an adventure," she said.

So did her fellow travelers, 13 other older men and women on a weeklong journey with Elderhostel, the nonprofit organization that arranges affordable, educational trips for people 55 and over.

Bypassing the more traditional, less physically challenging Elderhostel experience—studying the Civil War in New Orleans, say, or Mozart's operas in the Berkshires—they had left a world of comfort and ease to sit by the sea at the margins of the continent, pick salmon out of a net and bask in the light of the midnight sun.

As exhilarating as all that was, though, they were also on a journey that extended beyond geography and scenery. At a time in their lives when their hair was turning gray, they were traveling from a culture that worships youth and denies age to one that reveres its elders. Among the Inupiat Eskimos, who make up most of the population here, there are no senior citizens, no elderly, only elders. This is a place where old age is an achievement. Elders are to be respected. A highlight of the week was meeting Inupiat elders who had survived 60, 70 and 80 winters on this desolate strip of land.

"I'm proud of my gray hair and wrinkles," said Beulah Commack, an Inupiaq Eskimo elder nearing 70 who was the camp cook. "God made me this way."

---

1. Article by Sara Rimer from *New York Times,* September 2, 1998. Copyright © 1998 *New York Times.* Reprinted with permission.

Many things happened in this week. Men and women who did not know each other shared meals, jokes, stories and secrets—and the outhouse at the primitive fish camp that was their home base. No one talked much about the jobs or titles they had once held. These were people living in the present, looking ahead and thinking about what they wanted to do with the time they had left.

Dick Field, 68, from Tucson, Ariz., who volunteered for outhouse duty, had been a radiologist in Maine. He had loved practicing medicine, and retired with difficulty, but "I've fallen in love with my wife all over again," he said. His wife of 45 years, Ann, 64, had retired as an oncology social worker, but what she had always wanted to be, what she now had the time to be, in a way, was an anthropologist.

> *These were people living in the present, looking ahead and thinking about what they wanted to do with the time they had left.*

"You move on," Mrs. Field said.

Maryann Mendenhall asked, "Want to see a walrus head?"

Mrs. Mendenhall, a 69-year-old Inupiaq, had already told her Elderhostel visitors about the time she killed a polar bear. She had told them about toughing out winter in the days before electricity and snowmobiles. The visitors in her living room definitely wanted to see the walrus head.

Mrs. Mendenhall disappeared into the back of her house and returned dragging the huge skull of a walrus she had bagged some years ago.

"Can I try lifting it?" asked Ms. Wroe, a retired clinical director of physical therapy at the University of Florida. It was heavy.

Even if she was not a noted hunter, Mrs. Mendenhall would be an elder by virtue of her age.

"If you survived one year here, you could understand what it is to survive 70 years," said Ruth Sampson, 43, an Inupiaq who talked about the elders with the travelers. "Whether you're an Eskimo or white, you sure do command respect for your ability to survive winter in this cold and unfriendly environment."

As for death, like the endless winters, it is faced unblinkingly. In Kotzebue, the cemetery is next to the playground. "When your time comes, your time comes," Mrs. Sampson said. "You can't go over it, beside it or under it. You have to go through it."

All that the Elderhostel travelers had to survive was one week in mid-August. There are no roads into Kotzebue. Landing at the airport, they were met by a broken-down yellow bus with a cracked windshield, taped-up steering wheel and seats that slid off their frames around every bend in the unpaved road.

Six miles out of town, they came to a narrow strip of gravel beach with a jumble of drafty cabins, salmon cutting sheds, caribou bones and a couple of outhouses. On one side was Kotzebue Sound, feeding into the Chukchi Sea. On the other was tundra. Down the beach was a dead walrus. This was LaVonne's Fish Camp. LaVonne Hendricks, a commercial fisherwoman and former public health nurse, was their trip director.

All was far from ready. One cabin was empty, without a stick of furniture. A blackboard listing the day's chores included "Make Beds." A handyman eventually showed up with a hammer, nails and wood and made two beds. It would be a metaphor for the improvisational nature of the week. There was no schedule, Ms. Hendricks told them, "only possibilities."

"I thought, 'Omigod, what have I done!'" Ms. Wroe confided that evening, over group cocktails—cheap wine from a cardboard box.

The friend she had persuaded to join her, Claudette Finley, 59, had wondered the same thing. "I thought, 'I'm going to kill Martha Wroe,'" she said.

The state of the fish camp turned out to be an excellent icebreaker. Chuck and Martha Willis, from Dayton, Ohio, said they had broken their rule for Elderhostel trips. "We only look at the ones that have private baths," Mr. Willis said.

The Elderhostel travelers were to spend the week meeting Inupiat elders and experiencing their traditional way of living off the land and sea.

Over dinner—caribou soup and chum salmon, just caught —the talk of Elderhostel trips taken continued. Dick and Ann Field were on their eighth; they had watched whales off Baja California, explored American Indian culture at a Hopi reservation, dabbled in alternative healing in Montana.

From a handful of offerings at New England colleges with 240 participants 20 years ago, Elderhostel has grown so that its catalogue lists 10,000 programs that are attended by more than 300,000 people a year.

Lois Harris, 61, from Salem, Ore., who had just retired from nursing, had come with her cousin, Dorothy Parrott, 64, from Eugene. Mrs. Harris's husband, Ed, died seven years ago. Mrs. Parrott's husband, Glenn, died of a heart attack a year ago.

Mrs. Parrott was doing the dinner dishes on a table outside with two other women. "Glenn died the day after my birthday," Mrs. Parrott said. "It's like I've been cut, and a part of me is gone."

She pulled down the neck of her sweatshirt to reveal a tattoo, of a broken heart. "I got this six months after my husband died," she said. The women clasped her arm.

The Elderhostel travelers were to spend the week meeting Inupiat elders and experiencing their traditional way of living off the land and sea. That meant, for starters, going out on a boat to pick salmon off the net, then gutting it, drying it on racks and smoking it.

"I want everyone to have a direct relationship with a fish," Ms. Hendricks announced the first night.

Mr. Willis, a foundation executive, whispered to his wife, a retired nurse, that he was not going to touch any fish. Hours later, near midnight but with plenty of daylight left, he was on a boat near shore, up to his elbows in salmon.

The second day it rained. The group went on a tundra walk anyway. The tundra, a carpet of blueberries, crowberries, dwarf birches and wildflowers over a layer of permafrost, is spongy and difficult to walk on even when rain has not dotted it with knee-deep puddles.

Martha Wroe quickly fell behind, a small figure in an oversized yellow rain suit. The others kept stopping to see if she needed help, but she waved them on. Once or twice she fell. But eventually she caught up, at a lake where the group was watching a pair of Arctic loons.

"I was struck by the tundra," Mr. Field said in a group discussion after the walk. "I could have spent a couple of hours up there on my hands and knees," Mrs. Field added.

Bernice LaPorte, 66, who was on the trip from northern Maine with her husband, George, said: "The loons were spectacular. And the yellow canary."

Everyone gave a cheer for the canary, Ms. Wroe. Later, Ms. Wroe said: "I wanted to make it. I was thinking, What a thrill, here I am above the Arctic Circle, and I may never do it again."

As the week went on, the group met more Inupiat, at the fish camp or in their homes. The elders all had thoroughly modern bathrooms, the use of which they offered to their grateful visitors.

Growing older in a changing world, the elders from the lower 48 and those from the Arctic discovered they were dealing with many of the same things.

Esther Norton, an 85-year-old elder just back from three days of camping on the tundra to pick berries, complained that she had recently acquired a new house in town but her husband was refusing to move.

The Fields understood the conflict. Mr. Field would have liked to stay in Maine in retirement, but the Arizona climate was better for his wife's arthritis. "It was my turn to follow her," he said.

"We left a community where we were somebodies," Mrs. Field said. "Then you move to this large community where nobody knows who you are. It's humbling. It's scary."

And George LaPorte, a retired dentist who is an avid hunter and fisherman, knew how Mrs. Norton felt when she told the group, "I still feel young."

"I can't believe I'm 69," Mr. LaPorte said, flipping hamburgers on the grill one evening. "I can't believe I'm going to be 70."

Mrs. Commack, the camp cook, was moved hearing Mrs. Parrott talk about her late husband. Mrs. Commack's husband died three years ago. "I still miss my old man," she said.

And while the Elderhostel travelers worry about losing touch with younger people, the Inupiat in many cases face a greater divide. Their way of life has been sharply eroded over the last half-century by everything from missionaries to television to the tourists they were now entertaining.

"My children don't speak Eskimo," Mrs. Norton said.

But for all the commonalities, the Elderhostel visitors were all too aware of how different it was to be old in the lower 48. "I'm just starting to get this subtle feeling that I'm not as visible as I used to be," said Martha Willis, who is 62. "I'm getting a little less eye contact from the young, a little less consideration."

"I'm going to embrace the word 'elder,'" she said toward the end of the week. "I like it better than senior citizen."

What does it mean to be a senior citizen, anyway? "In the lower 48 it means getting discounts and things like that," Lois Harris said during a group discussion. "Here, it means self-esteem."

The weather itself was a test. It rained hard for five days. The waves reached the outhouse door. "My kids told me, 'Mom, get a new life,'" Mrs. Parrott said as the bus forded the flooded road on the way to town one day. She laughed. "I'm not sure this is what they meant."

The sun reappeared on the last evening. Mrs. Parrott and Mrs. Harris dipped their feet in the Chukchi Sea.

At a closing ceremony around the dinner table, everyone talked about what they would take away.

Mrs. Harris told the group: "This will help me with the journey I'm on. I'm 61, I'm still young. What am I going to do with the time I have left? What meaning can I find?"

Turning to Autobiography for Emotional Growth in Old Age[2]

By Sara Rimer
NEW YORK TIMES, February 9, 2000

The twice-monthly meeting of the writers' group was in session in the backroom of Fish Tales, a seafood restaurant across Seawall Boulevard from the Gulf of Mexico.

Bob Harvey, a mechanic who is 66 and twice divorced, rose from the table and read his latest poem, an ode to a long-ago love. Virginia Garvin, 78, a retired college English teacher, read a story about Navy boot camp in 1943.

Then Eleanor Porter, 75, who had been a magazine editor in Manhattan, took her turn. Her essay was an effort to explain the group: Why 21 men and women from their mid-60s to their mid-80s, who included a retired librarian, postal worker, accountant and former Roman Catholic priest, had been meeting for three years, writing their life stories and reading them aloud.

"This morning, as I was getting up, some lines came to me from a play," Ms. Porter said. "I thought it was *Death of a Salesman*. They go something like this. 'Attention. Attention must be paid to this man. He must not be allowed to drop into his grave like a dog.'"

"And I found myself thinking: That's what we are doing. We are paying attention to ourselves. We are paying attention to our lives. To what we have done and been and lived through."

This Galveston group is one of thousands across the country, in retirement communities and in nursing homes, on college campuses and in Elderhostels, in churches and synagogues, where older people are getting together to look back at their lives and share their stories.

The writing of autobiographies is hardly new, and the search for roots has been popular for some time. But now members of a reticent generation that came of age before the therapy culture and Oprah are excavating and disclosing their own personal histories— warts, secrets and all— examining the past to make the most of the years left to them.

"We've democratized autobiography," said Rick Moody, the former director of the Brookdale Institute on Aging at Hunter College. "It's no longer just for the rich and famous, for people with distinguished lives."

These new memoirists are writing for the same reasons writers have always written: to search for meaning in their lives, to find their voice, to leave a record.

"We're claiming our lives," said Ms. Porter, an exuberant woman who, in her writing, is working out why she never married, despite a number of proposals. "Your life is a bunch of stories, and then you put it down, and it has form. You think, 'This is my life, and it's O.K.'"

Gerontologists call the work these groups are doing by various names: life review, guided autobiography, spiritual autobiography, reminiscence. When done with a skilled guide and with sympathetic listeners, it can be a key to emotional growth in old age, they say.

Gerontologists call the work these groups are doing by various names: life review, guided autobiography, spiritual autobiography, reminiscence.

Bob Burdett, the retired accountant in the group, is writing his life story because he wants his three sons to have a record of who their father was. "My father just wasn't knowable," he said. "In my house, my mother did the talking. She had the feelings."

Dr. Moody said, "We're living in a world where people say, 'Oh, get over it, don't think about the past, just move on.' What life review is saying is, 'No, think about the past, work it through.'"

Experts widely believed it was unhealthy for the old to look back until the 1960s, when Robert N. Butler, director of the International Longevity Center in New York, published a seminal article on what he described as the natural process of life review among older people.

Rose Dobrof, a gerontologist at the Brookdale Institute, recalls that as a young social worker at the Hebrew Home for the Aged in New York, nearly 40 years ago, she was advised to stop asking the elderly Eastern European refugees there about their childhoods, and instead take them to the bingo room.

"Some of the staff said we shouldn't encourage people to reminisce; it made them depressed," Professor Dobrof said.

The Galveston group began with a "Share Your Life Story" workshop at the University of Texas Medical Branch that was attended by 12 people.

Bob Harvey, who had never written much of anything, was among them. At first, he said, he felt embarrassed by his lack of education. But as he began to write about what he had done, his view changed.

"It's made me admit that I've had a hell of a life," said Mr. Harvey, who has been a brakeman, a florist, a newspaper delivery man and a mechanic on tugboats and oil rigs. "I never thought about it before. Day to day, you do things. Things happen. I found out, I've been shipwrecked off the coast of California, barroom brawling in Alaska, shot at in Germany."

"A bunch of guys get together, and you tell war stories," he went on. "You embellish them, and you lie a lot. It's a lot of fun. It's male bonding, you could say. To talk about it seriously, I never did. Maybe I've reached an age where I can afford the luxury of being direct and honest and more or less sincere, without feeling like I need to apologize for it: this is what I was and what I did."

Mr. Harvey has also written about the scent of gardenias—his own Proustian moment—the former wife he still loves, and the day he made a pact with a rat that he would not kill another living thing unless absolutely necessary.

"Maybe I've reached an age where I can afford the luxury of being direct and honest and more or less sincere, without feeling like I need to apologize for it: this is what I was and what I did."—writing
group member Bob Harvey

The workshop was led by Thomas R. Cole, a professor of humanities in medicine at the Institute for the Medical Humanities at the medical branch, with one of his graduate students, Kate de Medeiros. Dr. Cole said he learned the power of narrative by writing the biography of Eldrewey Stearns, a manic-depressive recovering alcoholic who had been a leader in the sit-in movement in Houston in the early 60s. The book, *No Color Is My Kind* (University of Texas Press, 1997), was a collaboration, with Dr. Cole taping Mr. Stearns' recollections.

"It gave him back his life in a form that nobody could take away," Dr. Cole said.

Dr. Cole said the workshop was inspired by others in the field of aging, including James E. Birren, a leading gerontologist who teaches guided autobiography at U.C.L.A. and the poet Marc Kaminsky, who helps the elderly tell their stories through poetry.

Dr. Cole and Ms. De Medeiros encouraged the group's members to write in whatever form suited them.

"It's a very conscious shaping of turning points," Dr. Cole said. "What is it you need to work on? What is it you want to reclaim and narrate, to get clearer on?"

Reading to the group is as important as writing. "An idea is nothing till you put it down on paper," said Ivan J. Arceneaux, 71, who has written about the day shortly before his ninth birthday when he decided to become a priest. "Reading it is unbelievable. To read it aloud makes all the difference in the world."

Like many other women of her generation, Joy Weiss, 80, did not think she had anything to say. Her son, Marc, pushed her to join the group not long after her husband died, she said. "I said, 'Marc, what can I write about? I don't remember anything.'"

"I never had that much self-confidence," added Mrs. Weiss, who married young, worked in her parents' furniture store and reared three sons. "Other people have moved around and traveled and seen other parts of the world. All I know is Galveston."

But Mrs. Weiss found things she could write about—her mother, her childhood memories of nickel Cokes, her husband of 55 years.

"You would be proud to know that I have become a little more independent," she wrote in a letter to her husband, "realizing I am on my own and must assume certain duties. You should see me replacing batteries where needed and resetting the clocks and answering machine."

The point of the group is not simply to tell entertaining stories. "You can't just ask people for their happy memories," Dr. Cole said. "You've got to find out what's stuck in your craw. It takes courage."

Julius Halasz, 85, a Hungarian immigrant who says he spent his adult life "hiding from my memories," took Dr. Cole at his word. In *My First Christmas Present in the U.S.A.,* he wrote about the breakup of his marriage nearly 50 years ago, when his wife cheated on him and then left him for the other man.

"I got into my car, started to drive toward east, quite away from Toledo, practically numb, when it started to dawn on me what happened," he wrote. "It finally dawned on me what had happened, to me, who was so anxious to have a family and keep it together in any kind of condition. It was lost so easy, with a single cheap deception."

Mr. Halasz has also written about his parents, who were killed in World War II, and about the solitary life he led after his divorce, working all over the world as a construction engineer. "It comes in sequences back so clearly it's unbelievable," he said. "It reminds me how many times I went to sleep alone in my life. I looked up at the ceiling and say, 'Why me?'"

But Mr. Halasz also writes about the past decade, about his life with "my dearest," Velma Bradshaw Leavell, 84, a widow.

"When we first met, he didn't want to sleep with me because he was afraid he would hurt me," Mrs. Leavell said. "He slept so fitfully he thought he would hit me. I told him, 'Don't worry about it, I'll just conk you on the head.' After he started writing, he got less fitful."

Mrs. Leavell's autobiography, which she is writing for her four children and has her passion for horses as a major theme, is not without pain. "I just lived every day," she said. "I never even thought about it till we started writing about it. I lost a baby, lost a husband, lost another husband, my mother died. You learn to go with the flow."

Ms. De Medeiros has collected the groups' work into two books, published by the senior services office at the University of Texas Medical Branch. She is 35, and one of the things that has struck her is what older people choose to write about.

"They write about the relationships and the very small gestures that have made them human."—Kate De Medeiros, the Institute for the Medical Humanities

---

"No one, regardless of what they did for a living, ever writes about their jobs, or their weddings, or the birth of their children, or the war, things that many people would assume most older folks would write about," she said. "They write about the relationships and the very small gestures that have made them human."

Excerpts from the "Share Your Life Story" Group in Galveston

Eleanor Porter from "Share Your Life Story, Baby"

Proms are the presumably necessary rituals of the tribe, the trials by which the tribe sorts out the most obvious winners of the most obvious stakes: the sexual stakes. The hero athlete and the pretty cheerleader. Winners in the competition of reproductive genes. Proms do not measure intelligence, sensitivity, artistic merit, moral awareness, etc. . . .

In the sexual stakes game, I was lost and wandering. Try, in Galveston, Texas, in the south of the U.S. of A., in circa 1939, try being female, intense, bright, anxious and too tall. Then try making small talk in the spaces between partner dances. Try hell.

It's like not knowing how to groom, if you are a chimpanzee. You are out of it. And the tall, bright chimpanzee felt therefore repeatedly humiliated and repeatedly helpless, in a situation for which there was no solution, no way to work at the problem. Scholastic tests you could study for. Good behavior you could accept. Proms, you could only grit your way through . . . .

And then, a thousand years later, you are free at last. You have been loved, you have cried, you have been happy, you have lost, you have been in it and now you have personally influenced a dozen people to come to a little nightclub, a little cave, that has been there at 33rd and Ball for fifty years, reaching back to the glory days of entertainment in this little city, to when artists of entertainment came to the city auditoriums, and to the big clubs, the big caves, and then, later, to this tiny spot to relax and jam. . . .

We are suddenly dancing, free form, alone and together. We don't need partners. We are maturely sexual. We have evolved. First apes, then primitive man, then fast forward to the prom.

And then there is Ellie, a certain female in the tribe, observed by anthropologists to have been uncertain and sad at certain former rituals in the early years. She is observed screaming with wine-induced laughter, free at last, moving toward death with the happy beat. Moving on. Moving, baby. Moving.

Bob Harvey from "Night of the Rat"

There was light enough to read by if you don't mind squinting a little and it was by this light that I spotted my first victim. He wore a shiny, ebony coat as he calmly sauntered down the stringer toward the morning's repast I had placed about eight feet from my sniper's position.

I figured that when he became engrossed in gorging himself, I would send him to rat heaven, but he did the unexpected. Instead of immediately attacking his food, he sniffed it several times, picked it up in his mouth and with calm dignity, walked slowly toward me. I was absolutely awed when he stopped about two feet away, dropped his food, stood up on his hind legs and seemed to deliberately appraise me. . . .

In fascination I watched his post breakfast grooming ritual as he carefully washed his paws and combed his hair. It was during this process that he and I reached a tacit gentleman's agreement, the terms of which are as follows:

1. I would never again kill anything unless absolutely necessary. Necessary meaning to protect myself or to prevent or end a creature's suffering.

2. To kill without hesitation and as painlessly as possible.

3. Never to accept pleasure, satisfaction, or guilt from the justified killing of any living thing.

Bob Burdett, "What Now?"

Retired.
Off the treadmill.
Out of the rat race.
Affairs in order.
Paper read.
Bills paid.
Laundry washed and folded—
It'll only take a minute to put it away.
Enough time for everything—
Then some.
Too much of a good thing.
Too many crossword puzzles.
Too many naps.
Errands I used to do on the way from Point A to Point B
      have become major events.
Is this what it's supposed to be like?
I retired on insufficient data.
Now I'm expected to live another 25 years.
Almost 10,000 days.
A slow death.
Travel?
Romantic involvement?
Don't think so.
Need to do something productive,
Significant,
Meaningful,
Gratifying.
Like re-invent myself.
Start all over.

What Is Successful Aging?[3]

By Jimmy Carter
Excerpt from the Book *The Virtues of Aging*

Go out on a limb.
That's where the fruit is.

What should be our major goals as we prepare for our later years? You may be surprised to learn that I think one of the most important should be our own happiness. I don't consider this to be a selfish approach, because it will almost inevitably open up better relationships with others. It should be clear that happiness doesn't come automatically, but is something for which we must strive forthrightly, enthusiastically, and with imagination. We will fail if we just set a selfish goal: "I'm going to be happy!" So what is involved in enjoying our later years? I have read many studies that attempt to give us the answer.

Some sociologists have decided that the three most significant predictors of successful aging are (1) the level of education we have attained, (2) the amount of physical activity that we maintain, and (3) the degree of control that we feel we have over our own destiny. All these are important, but I don't agree that these are the ultimate criteria. For instance, let's assume that two men equally confident about their power to affect their own lives—a lonely college professor who runs five miles every day and a retired farmer who never attended college but has a cohesive and loving family and whose most strenuous exercise is hugging his wife several times a day. It is unlikely that the professor is either more successful or happier than the farmer.

Others believe that happiness depends on one or more good personal relationships and some involvement with a faith community, and the ability to extract from memories the positive things that give a sense of pride or at least the satisfaction of a worthy life. These are also good, but inadequate.

I'm inclined to agree with an elaborate study sponsored by the MacArthur Foundation, which concluded that the three indicators of successful aging are (1) avoiding disease and disability, (2) maintaining mental and physical function, and (3) continuing engagement with life. The latter involves keeping up relationships with

---

3. Excerpted from *The Virtues of Aging* by Jimmy Carter. Copyright © 1998 by Jimmy Carter. Reprinted with permission.

others and performing productive activities. This engagement in living—successful adjustment to the changing conditions we have to face—will inevitably involve us with responsibilities, challenges, difficulties, and perhaps pain. But these experiences will tend to keep us closer to others and allow us to develop more self-respect and mastery over our own lives—crucial elements for a good life.

Sigmund Freud summarized all these propositions by saying that the essentials of human life are work and love. These are much closer to my own beliefs, providing we can provide an adequate definition for both words.

... each of us is a complex human being, with multiple choices of our primary interests or identification at any moment. Keeping a number of these options alive is a good indication of the vitality of our existence.

We tend to feel that our work defines who we are. In our later years, if we are asked, "Tell me about yourself," we might respond, "I'm retired," and perhaps go on to explain what we used to be. At different times in my life I have introduced myself as a submariner, farmer, warehouseman, state senator, governor, or even president, if that was necessary. I might have added where I lived, but that was about it. Now, even though not holding a steady job, I could reply, depending on my audience, that I am a professor, author, fly fisherman, or woodworker. I could add American, southerner, Christian, married, or grandfather. The point is that each of us is a complex human being, with multiple choices of our primary interests or identification at any moment. Keeping a number of these options alive is a good indication of the vitality of our existence.

I think most of us who grew up on farms during the Great Depression have been stamped for life by the experience. We saw many neighboring families lose their farms and homes because of excessive ambition, the purchase of new equipment, planting too large an acreage, or not tending well what was planted. The fear of bad weather and the resulting inability to pay our crop mortgage was constant. We learned to live very cautiously.

My concepts of life were shaped by these memories, even when I had a secure job as a naval officer. I was extremely careful about the future. Our gross income was only $300 a month when I was on my first ship, but I bought a $50 savings bond and paid the maximum national service life insurance premium permitted, and we increased our savings rate as my salary was slowly raised. We didn't buy an automobile until I became a submariner, and then we committed all my hazardous duty pay to reduce this debt as rapidly as possible.

Later, when I resigned from the navy late in 1953, we qualified to live in a government housing project, where the rent was $31 a month. We used our small savings to invest in farm supplies to be sold in the Plains community. A severe drought in our area limited our total income to $280 during our first year in business, most of which was in unpaid customer accounts. Perhaps understandably, the local banks all refused to give me a loan to begin another year. Carter's Warehouse survived because our fertilizer supplier agreed to let me keep a small inventory if I paid them after I collected for the sales we made. We developed a profitable business during the following years, but I don't remember ever discussing at that time any plan for financial security in our old age, except that we would continue working as long as Rosalynn and I were physically able.

Instead of acting boldly and expanding my personal horizons, I was more inclined to concentrate on existing duties, do them well, and make cautious and incremental changes in my life's commitments.

One Sunday I taught a Bible lesson that really perplexed me, in that it violated the basic philosophy of our farming community. It was from Ecclesiastes: "Whoever watches the wind will not plant; whoever looks at the cloud will not reap." We had been taught to watch the wind and clouds, and always to accommodate the weather in planting, cultivating, and harvesting. As I tried to explain the text to my class, I finally realized that the writer was saying, "Don't be too cautious; take a chance! If you wait for perfect conditions, you may end up living a timid and diminished life. The prospect of failure always exists, and it is painful and often embarrassing when we do fail. But it's better to fail while striving for something adventurous and uncertain than to say, 'I won't try, because I may not succeed completely.'"

> *If you wait for perfect conditions, you may end up living a timid and diminished life.*

It wasn't much later that, perhaps influenced by these thoughts, I decided to run for the state senate. Like anyone else, I certainly failed sometimes when I took chances—in the navy, in business, and in politics. But I learned that even the failures force us to stretch our hearts and minds, and the successes more than compensate for the losses. This premise is particularly applicable to those of us who have reached retirement age. It is a time when we can, by default, live a passive and inactive life. But there is a wonderful, if riskier, alternative. We can take advantage of our new-found freedom and embark on new and exciting adventures. We now have time to fulfill some earlier ambitions. If we make a mistake, there are plenty of fallbacks. We need not be too cautious.

Bibliography

Books

Aaron, Henry J., and Robert D. Reischauer. *Countdown to Reform: The Great Social Security Debate*. New York: Century Foundation Press, 1998.

Achenbaum, W. Andrew. *Old Age in the New Land: The American Experience Since 1790*. Baltimore: Johns Hopkins University Press, 1978.

Angel, Ronald J., and Jacqueline Lowe Angel. *Who Will Care for Us?: Aging and Long-Term Care in a Multicultural America*. New York: New York University Press, 1997.

Austad, Steven N. *Why We Age: What Science Is Discovering about the Body's Journey Through Life*. New York: J. Wiley & Sons, 1997.

Beauvoir, Simone de. *The Coming of Age*. Translated by Patrick O'Brian. New York: Norton, 1996.

Butler, Robert N. *Why Survive? Being Old in America*. New York: Harper & Row, 1975.

Carter, Jimmy. *The Virtues of Aging*. New York: Ballantine Publishing Group, 1998.

Cassidy, Thomas M. *Elder Care: What to Look For, What to Look Out For!*. Far Hills, NJ: New Horizon Press, 1999.

Cole, Thomas R. *The Journey of Life: A Cultural History of Aging in America*. New York: Cambridge University Press, 1992.

Cole, Thomas R., and Sally A. Gadow, eds. *What Does It Mean To Grow Old?: Reflections from the Humanities*. Durham, NC: Duke University Press, 1986.

Comfort, Alex. *Say Yes to Old Age: Developing a Positive Attitude Toward Aging (Revised and Updated)*. New York: Crown, 1990.

Congressional Budget Office. *Long-Term Budgetary Pressures and Policy Options*. Washington, DC: Congressional Budget Office, 1998.

Costa, Dora L. *The Evolution of Retirement: An American Economic History, 1880-1990*. Chicago: University of Chicago Press, 1998.

Diamond, Timothy. *Making Gray Gold: Narratives of Nursing Home Care*. Chicago: University of Chicago Press, 1992.

Dychtwald, Ken. *Age Power: How the 21st Century Will Be Ruled by the New Old*. New York: Jeremy P. Tarcher/Putnam, 1999.

Dychtwald, Ken, and Joe Flower. *Age Wave: The Challenges and Opportunities of an Aging America*. New York: J. P. Tarcher, 1989.

Evaluating Issues in Privatizing Social Security. Washington, DC: National Academy of Social Insurance Panel Report, 1998.

Falk, Ursula A. *On Our Own: Independent Living for Older Persons*. Buffalo, NY: Prometheus Books, 1989.

Falk, Ursula Adler, and Gerhard Falk. *Ageism, the Aged, and Aging in America: On Being Old in an Alienated Society*. Springfield, IL: Charles C. Thomas Publisher, Ltd., 1997.

Freedman, Marc. *Prime Time: How Baby Boomers Will Revolutionize Retirement and Transform America*. First Edition. New York: Public Affairs, 1999.

Friedan, Betty. *The Fountain of Age*. New York: Simon & Schuster, 1993.

Furman, Frida Kerner. *Facing the Mirror: Older Women and Beauty Shop Culture*. New York: Routledge, 1997.

Goldberg, Beverly. *Age Works: What Corporate America Must Do to Survive the Graying of the Workforce*. New York: Free Press, 2000.

Gramlich, Edward M. *Is It Time to Reform Social Security?* Ann Arbor: University of Michigan Press, 1998.

Gullette, Margaret Morganroth. *Declining to Decline: Cultural Combat and the Politics of the Midlife*. Charlottesville, VA: University Press of Virginia, 1997.

Harris, Dan R., ed. *Aging Sourcebook: Basic Information on Issues Affecting Older Americans, Including Demographic Trends, Social Security, Medicare, Estate Planning, Legal Rights, Health and Safety, Elder Care Options, Retirement Lifestyle Options, and End of Life Issues*. Detroit, MI: Omnigraphics, 1998.

Hayflick, Leonard. *How and Why We Age*. New York: Ballantine Books, 1994.

Hudson, Robert B., ed. *The Future of Age-Based Public Policy*. Baltimore: Johns Hopkins University Press, 1997.

Kingsmill, Suzanne, and Benjamin Schlesinger. *The Family Squeeze: Surviving the Sandwich Generation*. Toronto; Buffalo: University of Toronto Press, 1998.

Kirkwood, Tom. *Time of Our Lives: The Science of Human Aging*. New York: Oxford University Press, 1999.

Lawrence, Martin M. *The Nursing Home Decision: Easing the Transition for Everyone*. New York: John Wiley & Sons, 1999.

Medicare and the American Social Contract. Washington, DC: National Academy of Social Insurance, 1999.

Moody, Harry R. *Ethics in an Aging Society*. Baltimore: Johns Hopkins University Press, 1992.

O'Brien, Raymond C., and Michael T. Flannery. *Long-term Care: Federal, State, and Private Options for the Future*. New York: Haworth Press, 1997.

Peterson, Peter G. *Gray Dawn: How the Coming Age Wave Will Transform America—and the World.* New York: Times Books, 1999.

Pipher, Mary. *Another Country: Navigating the Emotional Terrain of Our Elders.* New York: Riverhead Books, 1999.

Posner, Richard A. *Aging and Old Age.* Chicago: University of Chicago Press, 1995.

Powell, Douglas H. *The Nine Myths of Aging: Maximizing the Quality of Later Life.* Thorndike, ME: Thorndike Press; Originally published: New York: W. H. Freeman, 1998.

Quinn, Mary Joy, and Susan K. Tomita. *Elder Abuse and Neglect: Causes, Diagnosis, and Intervention Strategies.* New York: Springer Publishing Co., 1986.

Roszak, Theodore. *America the Wise: The Longevity Revolution and the True Wealth of Nations.* Boston, MA: Houghton Mifflin, Co., 1998.

Rowe, John W., and Robert L. Kahn. *Successful Aging.* New York: Pantheon Books, 1998.

Schiff, Harriet Sarnoff. *How Did I Become My Parent's Parent?* New York: Viking, 1996.

Suzman, Richard M., David P. Willis, and Kenneth G. Manton. *The Oldest Old.* New York: Oxford University Press, 1992.

Thompson, Lawrence H. *Older and Wiser: The Economics of Public Pensions.* Washington, DC: Urban Institute Press, 1998.

Williams, Mark E. *The American Geriatrics Society's Complete Guide to Aging and Health.* New York: Harmony Books, 1995.

Additional Periodical Articles with Abstracts

Those interested in reading more about the issues surrounding aging in America may refer to the following list of articles. Readers who require a more comprehensive selection are advised to consult *Reader's Guide Abstracts* and other H. W. Wilson indexes.

Will America Grow Up Before It Grows Old? Peter G. Peterson. *Atlantic Monthly* v. 277 pp55-8+ May 1996.

According to Peterson, America is headed for an all-engulfing economic crisis for which society is unprepared, and only drastic changes made now will enable it to be averted humanely. The author states that by 2013, when baby boomers will be retiring en masse, the annual surplus of Social Security tax revenues over outlays will become negative. The article suggests that a long-term budget balance should be achieved and guaranteed by the year 2002, entitlement programs should be reformed, working lives should be extended, a system of mandatory pensions or personal retirement accounts should be established, the tax base should be shifted from income to consumption, and a broad-scale public-education effort to promote saving should be mounted.

Baby Boomers at Midlife. David Masci. *CQ Researcher* v. 8 pp649, 651+ July 31, 1998.

This article examines the phenomenon of baby boomers who are fighting the aging process with remedies ranging from vigorous exercise to anti-aging hormones. Masci notes that some observers believe that these aging baby boomers are not facing the natural process of getting older in a mature way, and efforts to stay young will lead to disappointment.

The Myth of the Social Security Trust Fund. Ellen Frank. *Dollars and Sense* no. 223 pp19-23 May/June 1999.

Frank explains the system by which current surpluses in Social Security funds are piped into the federal budget and used to fund other government programs. The writer offers the opinion that since payroll taxes come predominantly from low and middle-income workers, the current excess payroll taxes should be used to fund government spending that benefits both the workers and the elderly.

The Quest for Youth. Scott Woolley. *Forbes* v. 163 pp146-51 May 3, 1999.

According to Wooley, virtually every drugmaker is tackling diseases or disorders that are connected to aging and marketers could make billions out of new sales to aging baby boomers who are motivated by an unprecedented intolerance for the aging process. However, employers and health plans might have to carry the cost of these developments. The article states that the quest for youth will give rise to some difficult questions regarding which treatments deserve coverage and whether the drugs will be abused by people who suffer more from vanity than illness.

Over the Hump. Erik Calonius. *Fortune* v. 138 pp108-114 Aug. 17, 1998.

Part of a special section presenting Fortune's 1998 retirement guide. The writer presents profiles of people who have devised ways to combine new careers with their passions in retirement.

Finished at Forty. Nina Munk. *Fortune* v. 139 pp50-4+ Feb. 1, 1999.

Munk examines the issue of maintaining employment over the age of 40. A recent study commissioned by the American Association of Retired Persons found that increasingly what matters to companies is potential, not experience. Moreover, Munk explainscompanies have less tolerance today for people they believe are earning more than their output deserves. This intolerance, or pragmatism, affects older workers more because the older an employee, the more likely he or she can be replaced by someone younger who earns half as much. Although a growing number of people in their forties are filing age-discrimination lawsuits, Munk states that suing for age bias is costly, emotionally draining, and rarely successful.

Hell No, We Won't Go! David Stipp. *Fortune* v. 140 pp102-6+ July 19, 1999.

In this article, demographer James Vaupel's prediction that one-half of the girls and one-third of the boys born recently in the developed world will be centenarians is explored. The factors behind the trend toward living longer and the disadvantages it brings are examined.

Today's Affluent Oldsters: Marketers See Gold in Gray. Carter Henderson. *The Futurist* v. 32 pp19-23 Nov. 1998.

According to Henderson, longer, healthier lives are resulting in a larger population of senior citizens, who are upending today's business marketing strategies. A growing number of companies are currently reexamining their businesses to see how they can capitalize on today's aging consumers. According to Census Bureau predictions, by 2030 the number of Americans over 65 will almost triple to more than 70 million, or one-fifth of the population. As a consequence, the United States is rapidly being transformed from a youthful to an increasingly mature society. The writer discusses industries that have risen to meet the opportunities afforded by this market.

Does an Aging Society Mean an Aging Culture? Peter G. Peterson. *The Futurist* v. 34 pp20-2 Jan./Feb. 2000.

In an article adapted from *Gray Dawn: How the Coming Age Wave Will Transform America—and the World*, the writer discusses the implications of an aging society. As the median age in the developed world increases, the characteristics of personal aging may eventually define the tone and pace of the culture at large. Thus, Peterson says, the greatest challenge for aging societies will be to find some means of replacing the energy and daring of youth while retaining the wisdom and experience of the old.

The Role of Government in "A Society For All Ages." Robert B. Hudson. *Health and Social Work* v. 24 no 2 pp155-60 May 1999.

The writer examines the role of Social Security in the U.S. According to Hudson, in the opinion of many conservatives, private sector mechanisms can be reintroduced to promote economic opportunity and security among older people. The writer states that it is the responsibility of liberals and progressives not to allow the debate over the future of social security to be constructed in this manner: The role of social insurance in U.S. life cannot be recast as dated, aberrational, and not in keeping with core U.S. values about society and security. The article states that although privatizers seek to portray Social Security as a prime example of public sector excess because well-off older people now receive benefits, advocates must point to social security's unmatched success in reducing poverty among older people.

Face the Music and Dance: There's more to longevity than just staying alive. Mark Matousek. *Modern Maturity* v. 42R pp42-6 Nov./Dec. 1999.

In an interview, 73-year-old psychologist James Hillman opines that a body-focused view of longevity has damaged American culture and the lives of older people. Hillman says, "When we see an old wall, an old teacup, an old tree— we appreciate these things precisely for their oldness, the increased beauty of their years and the memories they contain. Things seem to gain in value when they get old, whether or not they're useful or beautiful, but we deny this same appreciation to old people."

Reform Social Security. Robert Greenstein. *The Nation* v. 268 pp5-6 June 21, 1999.

In this article, the debate over the future of Social Security is discussed, including the steps taken to preserve it under the Clinton administration. Fears that Social Security could still become insolvent around the year 2055 if additional steps are not taken are addressed.

Perceptions of Aging in America. W. Andrew Achenbaum. *National Forum* v. 78 pp30-33 Spring 1998.

The author, a historian who specializes in the study of aging, recounts his father's admonishment that life experience alone enables us to understand the process of growing older. Here, Achenbaum summarizes several "universals" of aging. He states that old age "has always been considered the last stage of existence before death," older people "are more diverse than any other age group," and "attitudes toward age and aging are very mixed." He also divides the history of aging in America into three periods, up through 1935, when Social Security was enacted, thus ushering in what Achenbaum calls the "modern era of old age." Achenbaum predicts that the experiences of women and Hispanics will increasingly influence perceptions of aging, and organizations advocating the interests of older people will grow in prominence and work with other groups on behalf of pertinent issues.

As Centenarians Thrive, 'Old' Is Redefined. Sara Rimer. *New York Times* ppA1+ June 22, 1998.

Rimer looks at centenarians, who are proportionately America's fastest growing age group, with projections that by the middle of the 21st century, more than 800,000 people will be over 100. In fact, Rimer says, so many people are making it to 100 in relatively good health, as life expectancies in general shoot up, that centenarians, once sentimentalized rarities, have become symbols of the country's age boom and a metaphor for a dramatic shift in attitudes about what old means.

Home and Not Alone: A Foster Care Program for Grown-Ups. George James. *New York Times* sec. 14NJ p8 Nov. 29, 1998.

James describes services offered by Alternate Family Care, a New Jersey program that places seniors in foster care. The article describes one family that has opened their home to an older man; they feed and look after him in exchange for a modest monthly payment. According to James, the program benefits the participants, who get to select their home and often feel like part of a family; the caregivers, who supplement their income and get involved because they enjoy being with older people; and taxpayers , who would otherwise be spending more to provide nursing home care for people who did not require it, but had no where else to go.

Social Security: The Basics, With a Tally Sheet. David E. Rosenbaum. *New York Times* pA21 Jan. 28, 1999.

Rosenbaum reports that President Clinton's 1999 State of the Union Message, which proposed vast changes in the way Social Security is financed, touched off a hot policy debate. The article offers a primer on the basics of the program, its problems and its politics, and proposals by both Clinton and members of Congress to change it.

Pushing Limits of the Human Life Span. Gina Kolata. *New York Times* ppF1+ March 9, 1999.

The article focuses on a meeting of ten experts on aging who discussed whether human aging can be delayed, in light of the astonishing success scientists have had in recent years in increasing life spans of laboratory species such as worms and fruit flies. They say future generations may be able to avail themselves of scientifically established techniques to stretch the human life span until it reaches 150, even 200 years. Their goal is to allow people to be vigorous and healthy as they age, to stretch out good years rather than elongate ones spent in poor health. Fundamental questions remain unanswered, but the general direction of the research is clear. The scientists say what they have now is proof of principle and a staggering vision of future.

A Niche for the Elderly, and for the Market. Sara Rimer. *New York Times* pA1+ May 9, 1999.

Assisted-living facilities are spreading across America and now provide housing and an array of services to about 1.2 million people. The definition of assisted living varies widely from locale to locale among the nation's 30,000 assisted-living centers, and there is great variation in the services they provide and the fees they charge. Experts ask whether assisted living is a real solution for a new stage of life or a marketing opportunity directed at affluent elderly and their adult children. Some critics ask what will happen to assisted-living residents who run out of money or grow more disabled.

Making Your Way Through the Maze of Medicare Options. Larry Katzenstein. *New York Times* pH19 Feb. 16, 2000.

Katzenstein gives an overview of Medicare and related insurance programs, giving information about coverage provided by various plans and advice on which ones are generally appropriate for whom. Medicare was founded in 1966 in order to provide health insurance for American retirees, and all Americans over age 65 are eligible for coverage. However, Medicare alone does not pay for all the health care costs an individual is likely to incur, and thus other programs have sprung up to supplement its coverage. Options for additional insurance include plans provided by company retirement packages or, for seniors who work, by employers; Medigap policies, which are available from many insurers and supplement Medicare in varying degrees and at varying prices; and Medicare H.M.O.'s, which often provide more coverage than Medicare at only a slightly higher cost, but do not allow participants as much freedom in selecting doctors and hospitals.

Say Goodbye to the Office, Say Hello to Who Knows What. John A. Cutter. *New York Times* pH4 Feb. 16, 2000.

"These days, we seem almost born to retire," says an expert quoted in this article. According to the Social Security Administration, nearly 1.7 million Americans who were old enough to collect Social Security retired from jobs in 1999, in addition to thousands of younger retirees. Cutter recounts the last day on the job of one about-to-be retiree, and writes that when it is time to "walk out that office door for the last time, it can be a moment infused with feelings of anxiety and emancipation." While retirees look forward to spending their days as they choose, they also worry about boredom, financial security, and maintaining their health during the years to come. The retiree profiled plans to continue teaching a weekly class and doing volunteer work, and also hopes to travel and write a book.

Late-Life Unions: Not Too Late For Love. Bonnie Rothman Morris. *New York Times* (on-line) March 8, 2000.

Many older people are choosing to get married late in life, and such marriages are described by observers and the couples themselves as especially rich in companionship. Couples often use words such as "peaceful, gratifying, and liberating," in discussing their marriages. The individuals in these relationships are typically free from the pressures of working and raising families, and, due to their added years of life experience, are often highly aware of "what they are looking for in a mate." Difficulties may arise because of the concerns of adult children, who sometimes fear a new spouse will usurp their role in making decisions regarding care should their parent become sick, or that they may lose their inheritance to the new spouse. Some older couples consult lawyers or sign prenuptial agreements to alleviate such worries. New spouses may also feel burdened if their partner suffers a long-term illness early in the relationship. Despite these potential stumbling blocks, "many people in late-life marriages say they have never been happier."

These Roomies Share a House, and Old Age. Maria Newman. *New York Times* (online) March 8, 2000.

Many people age 65 and over are adopting a living situation more commonly associated with students and young professionals; namely, they are living with roommates in order to share expenses and companionship. Newman depicts one such household in New Jersey, the members of which say they enjoy the commraderie and added security the arrangement provides. The four residents, all of whom are healthy enough to care for themsevles, chose to live with roommates rather than with their families or alone. They were brought together by the Cooperative Housing Corporation, a New Jersey non-profit founded in 1986 that provides affordable housing for the elderly and disabled. While respecting each other's independence, the housemates are required to cook dinners for the group, and they provide each other with a sense of support. "It's nice to know you can call someone to help you," one resident said, as quoted in the article.

Building Wealth for Everyone. Daniel Patrick Moynihan. *New York Times* (online) May 30, 2000.

This editorial defends Senator Moynihan's plan to use a portion of the tax money that now funds Social Security to create personal retirement savings accounts for workers. He begins with a brief run-down of the history of social insurance, including the enactment of Social Security in the 1930s. In the 1970s, Congress added two percentage points to the tax that funds Social Security, which gave rise to surpluses that helped counteract the federal budget deficits of the 1980s and contributed to the federal budget surpluses of 1999 and 2000. Moynihan contends that with a few changes to the social security system, those two extra percentage points could be used to create optional individual retirement accounts for workers. The money would be invested as employees chose according to several different plans, based on the retirement plan currently available to federal employees. Upon retirement, they would then have access to the savings in these personal accounts in addition to, not instead of, their social security benefits, which would still be paid out by the government according to the same system in use today. Moynihan objects to the use of the term "privatization" to describe this plan, which was first proposed as a law in 1999, and which he believes would create a share of wealth for all American workers.

Can Human Aging Be Postponed? Michael R. Rose. *Scientific American* v. 281 pp106-11 Dec. 1999.

Part of a special section on what science will know in 2050. Antiaging treatments of the future will surely have to defeat many destructive biochemical processes at the same time. In the 1940s and 1950s, J. B. S. Haldane and

Nobelist Peter B. Medawar, both at University College London, first introduced the evolutionary explanation of aging, which held that aging appears in populations because natural selection, the watchdog that so fiercely protects traits ensuring strength during youth, itself becomes increasingly weak with adult age. Evolutionary theory and some basic experiments suggest that hundreds of genetically determined biochemical pathways—cascades of molecular interactions—influence longevity and might therefore be altered to postpone aging. As yet, only a few genes that could be involved have been discovered, however, mainly in the nematode worm Caenorhabditis elegans and the fruit fly Drosophila melanogaster.

Taking Care of Our Aging Parents. Cathy Booth. *Time* v. 154 pp48-51 Aug. 30, 1999.

The baby-boom generation must now deal with the issue of looking after parents who are no longer capable of looking after themselves. An unprecedented 13 percent of the population, or 33 million Americans, are over age 65, and this number will more than double by 2030. The number of Americans aged 85 and older has almost tripled since 1960, to 4 million, and will more than double over the next 30 years. Many parents have saved sufficient sums to afford to live in retirement communities or pay for full-time nursing care. The writer discusses her experience of caring for her mother, who suffered from Lou Gehrig's disease and died in 1996, and choosing an assisted-living facility for her father, who was recently diagnosed with Alzheimer's.

In the Long Run. Lee Smith. *Time* v. 154 pp Sept. 27, 1999.

Smith profiles five senior athletes who were preparing to participate in the 1999 National Senior Games, also known as the Senior Olympics. Held each year since 1987, in 1999 more than 12,000 men and women ranging in age from 50 into their 90s competed in sports such as track and field, swimming, volleyball, and archery. While many of these senior athletes are fiercely competitive, they also enjoy the camaraderie of participating in the games. Competitors are also proof of recent research on aging, which shows it is almost never too late to improve physical condition and performance. While there are some physical limitations inherent with age, the abilities of senior athletes are exceeding expectations of what was previously considered possible.

Can I Live To Be 125? Jonathan Weiner. *Time* v. 154 pp74-6 Nov. 8, 1999.

Part of a special section in which writers discuss their predictions for medical science and the environment in the next century. In the next century, new biological discoveries should mean that even more people will live to see old age and will encourage us to dream that we might not have to grow old at all. Seymour Benzer of the California Institute of Technology is searching through our genes for a kind of master clock that tells the body where it is in the line from cradle to grave and decides how fast we age. Benzer, 77, says that perhaps aging can be better described as a scenario that we can hope to edit, rather than as a clock. Humans are already making progress in preventive medicine and repairing old bodies—dealing with such things as abdominal fat, atherosclerosis, blood pressure, blood sugar, and cataracts. On the other hand, many biologists believe that aging and death are inevitable, and no one really knows whether human longevity will face a barrier that is fixed or one that is made to be broken.

The Stoic Way. Enrique Lynch. *UNESCO Courier* v. 52 p36 Jan. 1999.

Part of a special issue on the international aspects of longevity. Lessons about growing old gracefully found in the classical Greek philosophy of stoicism are discussed. Lynch writes, "The Greek philosopher Plato believed that philosophers are wise men who devote their lives to learning how to die and that philosophy, among other things, is a long and difficult process which teaches us to grow old and face up to the climactic moment of our lives." While in ancient times elders were valued for having attained "the age of reason in which the mind finally triumphs," today machines and computers teach us to value efficiency over wisdom, the author contends.

The World Turns Gray. Phillip J. Longman. *U.S. News and World Report* v. 126 pp30-5+ March 1, 1999.

Worldwide aging threatens global economic well-being. Although the world's population was doubling each generation in 1972, fertility rates are now at or beneath replacement levels in 61 nations, which represent 44 percent of the world's population. The cost of supporting a growing elderly population will put great pressures on the global economy: There will be fewer workers to support every retired person—rather than more, as was the case while birthrates were increasing—and markets will contract instead of expanding in substantial portions of the globe. Even given robust gains in productivity, a continuing shrinkage of the labor force might result in decades of falling economic output.

An Aging America Faces the Assisted Living Alternative. Keren Brown Wilson. *USA Today* (Periodical) v. 128 pp56-8 Mar. 2000.

The aging of America's population and the increased survival rates for those born with severe disabilities and those disabled later in life have led to a dramatic rise in the need for long-term care. The long-term care available for individuals has led to conflicts between some of America's most prized values, especially the desire to live independently and the need to be safe and secure. Assisted living has developed in response to those issues as an alternative way to cater to the needs of the frail elderly and disabled.

Immortality and Its Discontents. Sherwin B. Nuland. *Wall Street Journal* pA12 July 2, 1999.

Nuland argues that medical research should return to "the goal of preventing and treating the processes of degeneration that can begin at any age, but are most likely to hit the elderly." He begins by summarizing the advances in human longevity that have been made due to improvements in health care, the treatment of disease, and general awareness of healthy lifestyle choices. Furthermore, he continues, new research in the areas of aging and longevity, such as findings regarding telomeres, genes that control the aging process, and human embryonic stem-cell research, for example, promise to further extend the human life span. Nuland asserts that even should such efforts be successful, older people would still be likely to suffer from disease and disability. More traditional scientific and medical research, aimed at keeping people healthy, Nuland concludes, is more beneficial to society than that which aims to help people live longer.

A Caregiver Persists Despite the Indignities. Lorraine Adams. *Washington Post* ppA1+ Nov. 1, 1999.

As the ranks of the elderly continue to grow, finding and retaining nursing aides to provide one-on-one care is perhaps the single greatest problem facing the nursing home industry. Aides are prone to injuries resulting from lifting and moving frail patients, and are generally among the nation's lowest-paid workers. Due to these and other factors, the annual turnover rate for nursing aides is 93 percent. Furthermore, staff who are incompetent or who are simply too few in number are the chief causes of complaints regarding the level of care patients receive. Adams details the daily routine of one nursing-home caregiver who aspires "to be the best at what I do," as quoted by the writer. The intimacy that results from helping patients to conduct such basic activities as bathing and dressing is revealed, as is the stress involved in working with people who are suffering.

Rethinking National Retirement Policy: the Twenty-first Century Retirement Security Plan. Bradley D. Belt. *Washington Quarterly* v. 22 pp131-44 Winter 1999.

Part of a special section on the American Social Security program. The Center for Strategic and International Studies National Commission on Retirement Policy unveiled its landmark recommendations to strengthen the Social Security system and improve retirement security for all Americans in May 1998. The commission's Twenty-first Century Retirement Security Plan has been hailed as a benchmark for the debate on Social Security reform that will be taking place in the course of the year ahead, and it has been forecast that it will have considerable influence with the Clinton administration and on Capitol Hill. The plan is bipartisan, comprehensive, fiscally responsible, and bold. It offers a comprehensive approach to retirement policy that includes recommendations to strengthen the private pension system and enhance personal savings opportunities. Details of the plan's proposals in relation to the need to rethink national retirement policy are provided.

Index

DATE DUE

OCT 2 3 2007

NOV 1 3 2007

PLEASE DO NOT REMOVE THIS CARD FROM POCKET

PLEASE DO NOT REMOVE THIS CARD FROM POCKET

LIBRARY-LRC
UW COLLEGE MARSHFIELD
2000 W 5th ST.
MARSHFIELD WI 54449

DEMCO